the
tory
ted
Bad
n a
een

D1340637

Also by Colm Tóibín

COLM TÓIBÍN

Lady Gregory's Toothbrush

PICADOR

First published 2002 by The Lilliput Press Ltd, Dublin

First published in Great Britain 2003 by Picador
an imprint of Pan Macmillan Ltd
Pan Macmillan, 20 New Wharf Road, London N1 9RR
Basingstoke and Oxford
Associated companies throughout the world
www.panmacmillan.com

ISBN 0 330 41993 5

An abridged version of this book was published as an essay in the
New York Review of Books.

For permission to reproduce in its entirety 'Reprisals' by W. B. Yeats,
acknowledgement is due to A. P. Watt Ltd on behalf of Michael B. Yeats.

*The Lilliput Press receives financial assistance from An Chomhairle Ealaíon /
The Arts Council of Ireland*

1 3 5 7 9 8 6 4 2

A CIP catalogue record for this book is available from
the British Library.

Printed and bound in Great Britain by
Mackays of Chatham plc, Chatham, Kent

for Dympna Hayes

Contents

Illustrations

LADY GREGORY'S TOOTHBRUSH

In 1933, a year after her death, in his book *The Winding Stair and Other Poems*, Yeats published his two great poems about Lady Gregory. He described her old age in "Coole Park and Ballylee, 1931":

> Sound of a stick upon the floor, a sound
> From somebody that toils from chair to chair;
> Beloved books that famous hands have bound,
> Old marble heads, old pictures everywhere;
> Great rooms where travelled men and children found
> Content or joy; a last inheritor
> Where none has reigned that lacked a name and fame
> Or out of folly into folly came.

In "Coole Park, 1929" he contemplated Coole's legacy and the legacy of his old friend:

> *They came like swallows and like swallows went,*
> *And yet a woman's powerful character*
> *Could keep a swallow to its first intent;*
> *And half a dozen in formation there,*
> *That seemed to whirl upon a compass-point,*
> *Found certainty upon the dreaming air,*
> *The intellectual sweetness of those lines*
> *That cut through time or cross it withershins.*

The house is indeed gone, but there is no shapeless mound, there are no nettles. Coole did not meet the fate of other such houses in the period between 1918 and 1924. It was not burned; it was not attacked by the locals. It was sold to the Forestry Commission of the new Irish state, and in turn, after the old woman's death in 1932, it was sold to a local builder who demolished it. The site where it stood is now cemented over. But the famous tree where the famous carved their initials is still there, and it is still possible to make out the letters, from WBY and JBY to JMS and SOC and AE to GBS and, indeed, some others, less famous, both locals and visitors.

The house where Augusta Gregory was born, Roxborough, just seven miles away, was burned down in the Civil

War. Soon after the fire, on 8 October 1924, she went to look at it: "The house, the ruin is very sad," she wrote in her journal, "just the walls standing, blackened, and all the long yards silent, all the many buildings, dairy, laundry, cowhouses, coach houses, stables, kennels, smithy, sawmill and carpenter's workshop empty, some of the roofs falling in." "This is a sad day to the whole of us," Sean O'Casey wrote to her. "The ruins of all these lovely houses constitute a desolate monument of shame to Irish humanity." The estate Lady Gregory's family had run for many generations was divided into one hundred and twenty smallholdings, each, as one of her early biographers noted, "with its own neat grey box of a house".

She was born Augusta Persse in 1852, the youngest girl in a large family followed by four boys. In 1914, when George Moore in his autobiography attempted to suggest that she was "an ardent soul gatherer in the days gone by but abandoned missionary work when she married", she vehemently denied this in a letter to his publisher. "My mother and my two eldest sisters", she wrote, "thought it right to point out what they believed to be the different teaching of the Bible to that of the Catholic church to any Catholics who would listen. They made no secret of this proselytism which was much mixed up with benevolence and charity in those days, and my sister, Mrs Shawe-Taylor, especially, worked ardently for its accomplishment ... I myself, the youngest, shrank from any effort to shake or change the faith of others."

She was brought up in a strict and rigid Protestantism with much Bible-reading and devotion to duty. Her mother held strong views on what or who was unsuitable for her daughters. This included the reading of novels, and extended to John Lane, whom her sister Adelaide eventually married, and her cousin Standish Hayes O'Grady, the distinguished translator from the Irish, whom her mother, believing that cousins should not marry, banned from the house.

Lady Gregory's sisters were taller than her and had greater accomplishments in the art of finding a suitable partner. Augusta was considered the plain one, destined to be the carer, the spinster, whose type was depicted in *A Drama in Muslin*, George Moore's novel of Anglo-Irish decay set ten years later. In 1879, however, while accompanying her mother and her brother, who was ill, to Nice, she renewed her acquaintance with their neighbour Sir William Gregory, a widower, who owned Coole Park. He was thirty-five years older than her, he had been a member of parliament for both Dublin and Galway and had also been Governor of Ceylon. Unlike her own family, he did not farm his Irish estate or live fully on its proceeds. He lived mainly in London, where he was a Trustee of the National Gallery. He was interested in books and paintings and, when he came to Ireland, he gave her the run of his library at Coole. She read *Roderick Hudson* under his auspices, and *Middlemarch*. In 1880 she married him.

The house he took her to, and the life he gave her in their twelve years of marriage, and indeed his own connections and history, offered her a rich set of associations. At school in Harrow, he had sat beside Anthony Trollope. "He was a big boy," Sir William Gregory wrote in the *Autobiography* which Lady Gregory edited after his death, "older than the rest of the form, and without exception the most slovenly and dirty boy I ever met. He was not only slovenly in person and in dress, but his work was equally dirty ... These peculiarities created a great prejudice against him and the poor fellow was generally avoided ... He gave no sign of promise whatsoever, was always in the lowest part of the form, and was regarded by masters and by boys as an incorrigible dunce."

In the early 1840s, when Trollope was working for the Post Office in the Irish midlands forty miles from Coole, he renewed his acquaintance with Gregory and was a guest in the house. At twenty-five, Gregory had become an M.P. and was a great favourite among the political hostesses in London and indeed, for some time, was a protégé of Prime Minister Peel himself. "As Gregory's guest in Coole," Vic-

toria Glendinning has written, Trollope "listened to the social and political gossip and did not forget it ... It was the best possible fodder for a novelist ... It was the politics and the sexual scandals of the 1840s, when he knew almost no one, which were to be the starting-points for his fiction long after he left Ireland."

William Gregory introduced Trollope to many of the leading writers and politicians. Trollope repaid the compliment by using aspects of Gregory, his popularity and his promise in the London of those years, in the creation of the character of Phineas Finn. In 1875, when Gregory, to his own disappointment, had reached the pinnacle of his career as Governor of Ceylon, Trollope stayed with him for two weeks.

Despite the birth of their only child, Robert, in 1881, Sir William Gregory and his young wife spent a great deal of time in the 1880s travelling. They left their son at home, and this caused her much pain. Within a short time of her marriage she met Henry James in Rome, and later, in London, Robert Browning, Tennyson, James Russell Lowell, Mark Twain and many other writers and politicians and hostesses who were in Sir William's circle. Her accounts of those years are observant and wry. "I sat next to Henry James," she wrote, "and being in the middle of reading 'The Portrait of a Lady', asked why he had let Isabel marry that odious husband Osmond. He said she was bound to do something foolish, and I said yes with all that money. 'But without it,' he said, 'where would have been the story? Besides, it is delightful for a poor man being able to bestow large fortunes on his heroines.'"

Lady Gregory's most important and enduring relationship of those years began in Egypt in December 1881. Wilfrid Scawen Blunt, a handsome English poet and anti-imperialist, was travelling in Egypt with his wife, a granddaughter of Byron. Both couples became interested in Egyptian nationalism and especially in the fate of Arabi Bey, the Egyptian leader who sought a degree of freedom from the control which Britain and France exercised over his country. Blunt and Gregory began to write letters to *The Times*, whose editor was a friend of Gregory's, and their arguments went against the grain of British official policy. This made Blunt immensely happy. He loved foreign causes, but as the British government became more alarmed, Sir William, a pillar of the establishment all his life, slowly withdrew support. On 19 May 1882 Blunt wrote in his journal: "Gregory has failed us." Blunt continued to cajole, write letters and raise money. And Lady Gregory remained on his side. According to her diaries, Sir William said to her: "You and Wilfrid talk more nonsense than any two people settling the affairs of the world, and as old Mrs — said of the two English Commissioners sent to investigate the potato disease 'There isn't a hap'worth of sense in both your blocks.'" To win support for Arabi in England, Lady Gregory wrote an account of visiting his house and meeting his wife and children. Sir William gave her permission to publish it, and then withdrew permission as Arabi's forces were defeated by the British, and then restored permission when Arabi faced possible execution. It was her first published work, printed in *The Times* and later separately as a pamphlet.

The Gregorys spent the summers in Coole and the rest of the year travelling or in London. Lady Gregory kept a diary of her reading, she visited the poor, she enjoyed society. She remained an imperialist in these years, attacking Gladstone's assertion "that England without colonies would be as powerful as she is now" with elaborate argument. "He would probably also tell his gardener", she wrote in her notebook, "that a tree repaying by shade and shelter the nutriment drawn from the soil by its wide spreading roots would flourish and perform its function equally well if confined in a flower pot."

She seemed eager to impress Blunt and also to keep him at a distance, as he extended his anti-imperialist sympathies. In October 1883 she wrote to him: "Sir William writes to me from London that you are credited with having gone to India with the intention of overthrowing English supremacy and establishing Mahommedan rule and rapine throughout the peninsula, so I think you still have a chance of Tower Hill." From Coole she wrote: "The poor people come to the door daily, believing that I can cure them of all diseases, including poverty, and I mix their cough cures and buy their flannel and dye it with madder in an iron pot, and altogether I am at present one of the happy people without a history." But she did have a history, and as Blunt became more involved in the cause of Irish land reform, ending up in prison in Galway for his pains, her history gave them grounds for disagreement: "Called on Lady Gregory," he wrote, "who is growing very bitter against my politics, if not against me. It is curious that she, who could see so clearly in Egypt ... should be blind now that the case is between English landlords and Irish tenants in Galway. But property blinds all eyes, and it is easier for a camel to pass through the eye of a needle, than for an Irish landlord to enter the kingdom of Home Rule."

Sir William died in March 1892. Lady Gregory's tone in her journal entry in January 1893, when she remembered his death and his funeral, was grave, full of sharply remembered moments. "At Gort [near Coole]," she wrote, "the people met him at the train & carried him to the Church & went into the service — And next morning the tenants came, & attended service again, old Gormally kneeling by the coffin all the time — Snow was falling & there were few able to come from a distance — but all the poor were there." In between describing these events, she wrote: "Oh my husband! Do you know how little I have forgotten you!" By temperament and upbringing she was skilled in the art of "dutiful self-suppression", in James Pethica's phrase, and skilled too in the art of discretion. It is possible that nobody noticed anything special or peculiar in the twelve sonnets entitled "A Woman's Sonnets" which Wilfrid Scawen Blunt published at the end of January 1892, just over six weeks before Sir William Gregory's death. In his diary he wrote: "I have remodelled Lady Gregory's twelve sonnets, which I heard from her a day or two she would like to see printed in the new book, though of course without her name. They are really most touching and required little beyond strengthening here and there a phrase and altering a few recurrent rhymes."

Her sonnets make clear that she was in love with him and that she had an affair with him which began during their Egyptian sojourn, when she had been married for less than two years, and ended eighteen months later. Her image after Sir William's death was that of a dowager who exuded dryness and coldness and watchfulness, who wore black and modelled herself on Queen Victoria. The sonnets, on the other hand, disclose someone else:

> *If the past year were offered me again,*
> *And the choice of good and ill before me set*
> *Would I accept the pleasure with the pain*
> *Or dare to wish that we had never met?*
> *Ah! Could I bear those happy hours to miss*
> *When love began, unthought of and unspoke —*
> *That summer day when by a sudden kiss*
> *We knew each other's secret and awoke?*

In these twelve poems she was in the sweet position of disclosing the love which had to remain secret:

> *Pleading for love which now is all my life —*
> *Begging a word that memory may keep,*
> *Asking a sign to still my inward strife,*
> *Petitioning a touch to smooth my sleep —*
> *Bowing my head to kiss the very ground*
> *On which the feet of him I love have trod,*
> *Controlled and guided by that voice whose sound*
> *Is dearer to me than the voice of God.*

Very few of the changes Blunt made to the poems improved them; he tended to soften her directness and dull her precision. But he could do nothing to lessen the sense of loss and shame in some of these poems, which are quoted here in her versions:

> *Should e'er that drear day come in which the world*
> *Shall know the secret which so close I hold,*
> *Should taunts and jeers at my bowed head be hurled,*
> *And all my love and all my shame be told,*
> *I could not, as some women used to do*
> *Fling jests and gold and live the scandal down —*
> *I could not, knowing all the story true*
> *Hold up my head and brave the talk of town —*
> *I have no courage for such tricks and ways,*
> *No wish to flaunt a once dishonoured name —*
> *Have still such memory of early days*

And such great dread of that deserved shame
That when it comes, with one all hopeless cry,
For pardon from my wronged ones, I must die.

The ten years in Lady Gregory's life between the death of her husband in 1892 and the first performance of *Cathleen Ni Houlihan* involve what is ostensibly a complete transformation in her life. A landlord's daughter and widow, steeped in the attitudes of her class, she became an Irish nationalist and leader of a cultural movement that was more powerful than politics. But her activities in these ten years also displayed what would, for the rest of her life, range from ambiguities to deep divisions in her loyalties and her beliefs. In 1893, for example, she published in London an anonymous pamphlet called *A Phantom's Pilgrimage or Home Ruin*, essentially a piece of pro-unionist rhetoric, in which Gladstone returns from the grave ten years after Home Rule to find that every class in Ireland has suffered dire consequences. Later that year she travelled alone to the Aran Islands, staying in a cottage in Inishere "among people speaking scarcely any English". She wrote to English friends about the trip and her reading of Emily Lawless's novel *Grania*, set on the islands, and Jane Barlow's *Irish Idylls*, stories of Irish peasant life. ("I look on it as one of my Irish sermon books; it really gives me sympathy with the wants of the people.") In the meantime, she worked on her husband's incomplete manuscript for his *Autobiography*.

While this work seemed to Wilfrid Scawen Blunt merely a widow's "pious act", and had very many dull moments and displays of Sir William's self-importance and vanity, it was at the same time a piece of careful re-positioning and re-invention which would become the basis not only for Lady Gregory's life at Coole and her work with Yeats, but also for many of Yeats's poems about Coole and many of his Anglo-Irish attitudes. It would emphasize, as in her account of Sir William's funeral, that he was loved by the people, that he and his family were respected as landlords. She would insist upon this all her life. In her own conclusion to the book, she quoted from a letter he had written to her "just before our marriage": "I always felt the strongest sense of duty towards my tenants, and I have had a great affection for them. They have never in a single instance caused me displeasure, and I know you can and will do everything in your power to make them love and value us." She continued: "He was glad at the last to think that, having held the estate through the old days of the Famine and the later days of agitation, he had never once evicted a tenant. Now that he has put his harness off I may boast this on his behalf. And, in the upheaval and the changing of the old landmarks, of which we in Ireland have borne the first brunt, I feel it worth boasting that among the first words of sympathy that reached me after his death were messages from the children of the National School at Coole, from the Bishops and priests of the dio-cese, from the Board of Guardians, the workhouse, the convent, and the townspeople of Gort." In a letter to a friend of his in London composed while she was working on the manuscript, she wrote: "I attach great importance to the breadth and sincerity of his views on Irish questions being remembered."

This note would surface again and again in her letters and diaries. As late as 1920, when she was negotiating the sale of land at Coole, she wrote to Sir Henry Doran of the Congested Districts Board: "May I draw your attention to the fact that through all the troublesome times of the last forty years we have never had to ask compensation from the County or for police protection. We have been, in comparison with many other Estates, a centre of peace and goodwill. This was in part owing to the liberal opinions and just dealing of my husband and my son."

In the table of contents for Sir William's autobiography, Chapter VII contains a section entitled "The Gregory Clause". Sir William devoted two and a half pages to the subject, most of it a quotation from an article published in the *Dublin University Magazine* in 1876 that attempted to justify the Gregory Clause, which was passed by the House of Commons in March 1847.

Sir William Gregory was one of a large number of Irish landowners and politicians who took the view that the system of land-holding that had been in place in Ireland before the Famine could not continue. They believed that there were too many smallholdings and too many tenants.

In 1848, Lord Palmerston, for example, wrote to Lord John Russell: "It is useless to disguise the truth that any great improvement in the social system of Ireland must be founded upon an extensive change in the present state of agrarian occupation, and that this change necessarily implies a long, continued and systematic ejectment of small holders and squatting cottiers." During the first two months of 1847, in the House of Commons debates on the famine in Ireland, Sir William Gregory had argued against the system of relief being used. He supported the idea of assisted emigration. He also proposed an amendment to the Poor Law Act in March 1847 that was to have far-reaching implications. The clause stipulated that no one who held a lease for more than a quarter of an acre of land should be allowed to enter the workhouse or to avail of any of the relief schemes. This meant that a cottier tenant whose potato crop had failed a second year in succession and who had no money to buy food would be faced with a stark choice. If he wanted to take his family into the work-house, the only place where they could be fed, he would have to give up his lease and he would never get it back. His mud cabin would be razed to the ground as soon as it was empty. If he and his family survived the workhouse, where disease was rampant, they would have nowhere to go. They would have to live on the side of the road, or try to emi-grate. Nor could a man send his wife and children into the workhouse and stay on the land himself. They could get no relief unless he gave up the lease. "Persons", Sir William said in the House of Commons, "should not be encouraged to exercise the double vocation of pauper and farmer."

In his autobiography, Sir William quotes the *Dublin University Magazine* article from 1876 to justify himself: "That this clause has been perverted to do evil no one can deny, and those who only look to one side of the question have often blamed its author for some of the evils that were inflicted by its provisions ... The evil results we have alluded to were not foreseen, certainly they were not believed in by Mr Gregory, whose advocacy of the emigration clause is the best proof of his good motives to those who do not know the humanity and the kindness which, then and always, have marked his dealing with his tenants on his own estates."

The effects of the clause, however, were foreseen by those who voted for it in the House of Commons on the night of 29 March 1847, as well as by the nine MPs who voted against it. Sir William's proposing speech was followed by William Smith O'Brien, who was reported as saying: "If a man was only to have a right to outdoor relief upon condition of his giving up his land, a person might receive relief for a few weeks and become a beggar for ever. He thought this was a cruel enactment." Another speaker in the same debate said that the consequence of Sir

William Gregory's clause "would be a complete clearance of the small farmers of Ireland – a change which would amount to a perfect social revolution in the state of things in that country … to introduce it at once would have the effect of turning great masses of pauperism adrift on the community." Hansard reported that Mr Bellew, speaking in support of the clause, argued that it "would tend to the gradual absorption of the small holdings now so extensively held, as well as the conversion of masses of starving peasantry into useful and well-paid labourers". And Sir G. Grey in the same debate said that he "had always understood that these small holdings were the bane of Ireland".

In his autobiography, Sir William wrote: "There is no doubt but that the immediate effect of the clause was severe. Old Archbishop MacHale never forgave me on account of it. But it pulled up suddenly the country from falling into the open pit of pauperism on the verge of which it stood. Though I got an evil reputation in consequence, those who really understood the condition of the country have always regarded this clause as its salvation."

The Gregory Clause radically reduced the number of small tenants. Roughly two million people left Ireland permanently between 1845 and 1855, according to the historian Oliver MacDonagh, who also wrote: "The cottier class had virtually disappeared. The number of holdings under one acre had dropped from 134,000 to 36,000 ... the number of persons per square mile ... had fallen from 355 to 231; and the average productivity had risen greatly. In short, the modern revolution in Irish farming had begun."

Sir William's father died of fever during the Famine, and he himself witnessed the suffering around Coole and wrote about this in his book. "I did ... all I could to alleviate the dreadful distress and sickness in our neighbourhood. I well remember poor wretches being housed up against my demesne wall in wigwams of fir branches ... There was nothing that I ever saw so horrible as the appearance of those who were suffering from starvation. The skin seemed drawn tight like a drum to the face, which became covered with small light-coloured hairs like a gooseberry. This, and their hollow voices, I can never forget." In April 1847, four thousand destitute labourers gathered at Gort, the nearest town to Coole, looking for work. A year later, a Poor Law inspector wrote that he could scarcely "conceive a house in a worse state or in greater disorder" than the workhouse in Gort. A quarter of the population in the area sought relief in those years.

No one denied Sir William's personal concern about his tenants during the Famine, but the Poor Law clause he proposed in the House of Commons became one of the main causes of suffering in Ireland in those years. The importance of the Gregory Clause was emphasized during Sir William's lifetime by Canon John O'Rourke, author of the first history of the Famine, which was published in 1874 and remained in print as the only serious account for many years. Canon O'Rourke wrote: "A more complete engine for the slaughter and expatriation of a people was never designed ... Mr Gregory's words – the words of a liberal and pretended friend of the people – and Mr Gregory's clause – are things that should be forever remembered by the descendants of the slaughtered and expatriated small farmers of Ireland."

Sir William's "evil reputation" was as much a part of the legacy of Coole as his good name as a landlord. His famous clause helped to undermine the very class that Yeats and Lady Gregory later sought to exalt. Neither Yeats nor Lady Gregory wrote plays or poems about the Famine. It was not part of the Ireland they sought to celebrate or lament or dream into being. And there is something astonishing in the intensity with which Yeats sought to establish Coole Park and its legacy as noble, with "a scene well set and excellent company",

> *Where none has reigned that lacked a name and fame*
> *Or out of folly into folly came.*

Lady Gregory's response to her ambiguous legacy is fascinating. There was nothing impetuous in her nature. In the years after she had edited her husband's autobiography, she began to learn the Irish language, she went once more to the Aran Islands, and she began to study Irish history in order to edit the letters of Sir William's grandfather. Gradually, her unionist sympathies dissolved, disappeared. The transformation was slow. She did not go the way of other women of her class such as Constance Gore-Booth or Maud Gonne. She did not become a firebrand or a revolutionary. Her personality was calm and steadfast, and there was an odd wisdom in the way she lived after the death of Sir William. She loved Coole and she wished to remain true to her husband's memory and keep the estate and the house in order until Robert, her only child, could come into his inheritance. And slowly she began to love Ireland also, in the way that other nationalists of her time loved Ireland, inventing and discovering a rich past for her, and imagining a great future, and managing to ignore the muddy and guilt-ridden history in between this ancient glory and the time to come.

She was intelligent enough to manage the contradictions in her position, to allow her own response to her heritage to remain natural and easy. Fortunately, she was not introspective. She lacked vanity and this preserved her from too much self-examination.

She gave part of herself up to re-inventing Ireland. "Irish", she would write, "is the most ancient vernacular literature of modern Europe." In these last years of the nineteenth century she discovered that the "great bulk of [Irish] literature is certainly older than the twelfth century, but we can carry it back much farther, certainly to the sev-

enth century. The Cuchulain stories were put into perma-
nent literary form at about the same date as *Beowulf*, some
100 to 200 years before the Scandinavian mythology crys-
tallised into its present form, and at least 200 years before
the oldest Charlemagne Romances, and probably 300 years
before the earliest draft of the Nibelungenlied."

Her old friends began to notice the change in her.
After the publication in 1898 of *Mr Gregory's Letter-Box*, the
correspondence of her husband's grandfather, Sir Frederick
Burton told her that he saw a tendency to Home Rule on
her part. "No, not Home Rule," she replied, "but I defy
anyone to study Irish history without getting a dislike and
distrust of England." She began to defend her new self to
her friends. In a diary entry in 1900, she wrote about a dinner party with members of the establishment: "At dinner I
had a fight for the Irish language. Lord Morris says that he
never spoke against its being taught in the schools, for he
never heard any proposal at all being made for it at the
Board:— if he had he would only have laughed at such an
absurd craze. Lecky, defending his Trinity professors,
sneered at me for calling Irish a modern language. I said
yes, just in the same way as modern Greek; and Lady Morris told him it is spoken all around Spiddal."

In February 1898, however, when Yeats told her that
Maud Gonne was inciting hungry tenants in Kerry to kill
their landlords and seize food, Lady Gregory reverted to

her role as property-owner: "I was aghast and spoke very strongly, telling him first that the famine itself was problematic, that if it exists there are other ways of meeting it, that we who are above the people in means and education, ought, were it a real famine, to be ready to share all we have with them, but that even supposing starvation was before them it would be for us to teach them to die with courage than to live by robbery."

Lady Gregory first saw W.B. Yeats in the spring of 1894, as she noted in her diary: "at Lord Morris' met Yates [*sic*] looking every inch a poet, though I think his prose 'Celtic Twilight' is the best thing he has done". In the summer of 1896 she met him again when he was staying with Arthur Symonds at Edward Martyn's house, which was close to Coole. "As soon as her terrible eye fell upon him," Symonds later said, "I knew that she would keep him." She invited Martyn's house-party to Coole and invited Yeats to return. When he came again to Edward Martyn's house the following summer, both he and Lady Gregory were fresh from protesting against Queen Victoria's jubilee, he by walking in a procession in Dublin in the company of Maud Gonne behind a coffin with the words "British Empire" inscribed on it, she by refusing to light a bonfire, much to the disgust of her neighbours and friends the Goughs, "on the grounds of the Queen's neglect of the country". On a rainy afternoon that summer in a neighbour's house Yeats and Lady Gregory began the conversation that resulted in the Abbey Theatre.

She had a typewriter and servants and a big house. She typed out letters to the great and the good seeking support for their theatre. She began to collect folklore in the immediate area ("An old man in the workhouse", she wrote, "has a long poem but very few teeth, and the Moycullen priest, an Irish expert, is coming to help me interpret it tomorrow"); she offered Yeats two hundred thousand words for his use, which he put into shape and considered his own and published under his own name in six long essays. She later wrote with great reverence about folklore collecting: "It was a changing of the table of values, an astonishing excitement ... It was not to the corners of newspapers or even to the Broadsheets of ballads sung in the little towns I looked now for poetry and romance, it was to stone-breakers and potato-diggers and paupers in the workhouse and beggars at my own door." Others were not as reverent about her activities among the people in those years. The writer Brinsley MacNamara wrote that she gathered "material for her books and plays in the cabins and cottages of Clare-Galway, where she had been industriously plied with folklore specially invented for her visits, and all of which she had innocently accepted".

In the early years of their relationship, Yeats had a sense of her practical and dutiful nature, but none of her talent. She dreamed that she had been writing some articles, and that Yeats had said to her: "It's not your business to write. Your business is to make an atmosphere." Her life as a writer began slowly and tentatively. It began with her writing out the stories she heard in the area around Coole.

Her folklore collecting was not part of an unusual ambition, nor was her urge to create popular, or readable, versions of the ancient sagas. Her best friend in London, Lady Layard, who had given her the gift of her typewriter, was the daughter of Lady Charlotte Guest, who had made a readable and popular translation of the Welsh epics known as *The Mabinogion*. In 1878 her cousin Standish James O'Grady published his *History of Ireland: The Heroic Period*, in which he told the story of the sagas: "The forefront of Irish History we find filled with great heroic personages of a dignity and power more than human ... Century after century the mind of the country was inflamed by the contemplation of these mighty beings whom ... men believed to be their ancestors." In 1892 Standish Hayes O'Grady, also her cousin, had published his *Silva Gadelica*, which included translations from ancient Irish sagas that were stilted and literal but accurate. Lady Gregory had met during her years in London figures such as Edward Clodd, who wrote about the power of ancient stories, and Alfred

Nutt, who had published in 1900 a tiny pamphlet called *Cuchulain, The Irish Achilles*. For further reading, Nutt suggested Eleanor Hull's *The Cuchulain Saga in Irish Literature*.

In the second half of the nineteenth century, the study of an ancient Ireland had become part of the cultural life of certain (and indeed uncertain) Irish Protestants. Both of Oscar Wilde's parents had collected folklore or studied archaeology. It was part of the harmless idealization of the Irish landscape that is also to be found in the painting of the period, and in the songs of Thomas Moore. (It was part of the invention of tradition that also occurred in Scotland and Wales as traditional forms of life began to disappear.) Oscar Wilde's mother's extreme nationalism was unusual; most of the antiquarians, including both O'Gradys, remained unionists or apolitical. But this began to change in the 1890s. In 1898 Lady Gregory, through Yeats, met Douglas Hyde, who had founded the Gaelic League as a non-political organization aiming to revive Gaelic culture, but who remained alert to the political implications of such a revival. The Gaelic League, Hyde wrote to Lady Gregory, aimed "at stimulating the old peasant popish aboriginal population".

Hyde spoke Irish and translated songs and poems and stories, but he also enjoyed landed-gentry pastimes such as shooting at birds. Lady Gregory later wrote that when some ladies heard that a gentleman, namely Hyde, "had been talking Irish to the beaters while shooting with us said that was nonsense because no one who spoke Irish could be a gentleman. They also had never heard the language had the dignity of a literature."

In February 1900, as a result of pressure from the Gaelic League to introduce Irish as a school subject, Professor Robert Atkinson of Trinity College in Dublin wrote a report which stated that Irish literature "has scarcely been touched by the movements of the great literatures; it is the untrained popular feeling ... My astonishment is that through the whole range of Irish literature that I have read (and I have read an enormous range of it) the smallness of the element of idealism is most noticeable ... And as there is very little idealism there is very little imagination ... The Irish tales are devoid of it fundamentally."

In that same year an English editor asked Yeats to write a version of these sagas, but he refused, saying that he did not have the time. When Lady Gregory suggested that she might do a translation, Yeats was not enthusiastic; he had no confidence in her literary skills. But she set to work, and when she showed him a section she had done, he changed his mind and encouraged her. Yeats, she later wrote, "was slow in coming to believe I had any gift for writing and he would not encourage me to it, thinking he had made better use of my folk-lore gathering than I could do. It was only when I had read him one day in London my chapter 'The Death of Cuchulain' that he came to look on me as a fellow writer." Her aim was to refute Atkinson, to produce a version of the Cuchulain story that would display all its ingenuity and intricacy but also would be accessible to the general public. She thought it "might be used as a school book", which meant that she took great care not to include material that would shock the prudish. Much had been published over the years in fragmentary form; Lady Gregory now sought to stitch it together, making use of earlier translations, so that as a narrative it would make sense; she invented an idiom for it which was neither a direct translation nor standard English. She translated it into the English of Kiltartan, she said, the area around Coole, but much of it, in fact, is quite plain and natural, almost neutral in its tone.

Lady Gregory was nervous about the reception of *Cuchulain of Muirthemne* and about her own credentials as a translator. On 9 January 1902 she wrote to Yeats about his proposed introduction: "Whatever you write will be beautiful, but I don't think you need write much, the chief thing is to show that you, representing the literary movement, accept the book, and that it is not rubbishy amateur work, as critics might be prepared to think." His introduction was grandiloquent. It began: "I think this book is the best that has come out of Ireland in my time." He wrote about the language of the translation: "As she moved about among her people she learned to love the beautiful speech of those who think in Irish, and to understand that it is as true a dialect of English as the dialect that Burns wrote in. It is some hundreds of years old and age gives a language authority."

She dedicated her translation to the people of Kiltartan. The page-long introduction managed a number of astonishing false notes, as though Lady Gregory had been caught halfway in the act of self-invention. In attacking Professor Atkinson, the mistress of Coole left herself open to mockery: "And indeed if there were more respect for Irish things among the learned men that live in the college in Dublin, where so many of these old writings are stored, this work would not have been left to a woman of the house, that has to be minding the place, and listening to complaints and dividing her share of food." She mentioned at the end of the dedication that the people of Kiltartan "have been very kind to me since I came over from Kilcriest, two-and-twenty years ago". For a moment, Roxborough, with its English colonial sound, was being wiped off the map. The place she came from, in this final sentence, would have an Irish name.

She would also create a past for herself, much as Yeats would do, a heritage that did not include rent-collecting and proselytizing Protestantism and three brothers who died from drink. In her dedication, she mentioned a figure who would emerge as central in her version of her past. "I have told the whole story in plain and simple words," she wrote, "in the same way my old nurse Mary Sheridan used to be telling stories from the Irish long ago, and I a child at Roxborough." In her memoirs she would also invoke the spirit of Mary Sheridan, whom she claimed to have overheard talking to a beggar woman about their memory of the French arriving in Killala, Co. Mayo, sixty years earlier, in 1798. "And a child of the Big House", she wrote, "keeps a clear memory of the old, old nurse in earnest talk on the doorstep with an old, old beggar, each remembering, through near a century, the landing of the French in that year to help the rebels." Mary Sheridan, Lady Gregory wrote, had previously worked for Hamilton Rowan, one of the leaders of the 1798 rebellion.

This invocation of an old, old past would leave out most of her ancestors but would include Lady Gregory's great-grandfather William Persse, a member of the Volunteers who sought greater autonomy for Ireland in the 1780s. The Volunteer Bridge near Roxborough had a plaque in his memory: "This bridge was erected in 1789 by William Persse, Colonel of the Roxborough Volunteers in memory of Ireland's Emancipation from Foreign Jurisdiction." In re-creating herself, she moved from claiming a background that was connected to Irish rebellion to writing in support of rebellion itself. In the May 1900 edition of the *Cornhill* magazine, in an article called "Felons of Our Land", she wrote about the ballads and poems of Irish rebellion with great naïveté, praising the literature of rebellion with the unrestrained approval of the recently converted. The fate of the Manchester martyrs, she wrote, "gave the touch of pathos that had been wanting to the Fenian movement". She included some lines written by Blunt while in jail in Galway and inscribed on a book for her as an example of an old Irish ballad. In those years, as she re-made herself, anything could become part of the useful past.

She was in Rome when the magazine came out. An old friend of her husband who read the article scolded her, as she put it, for "going so far from the opinions of my husband and son". She wrote in her diary: "I had determined not to go so far towards political nationality in anything I write again, because I wish to keep out of politics and work only for literature; and partly because if Robert is Imperialist, I don't want to separate myself from him." The publication of her article did not prevent her and her son from being entertained at the British Embassy in Rome.

It would be easy to suggest that Lady Gregory's activities in these years are tinged with a sort of hypocrisy or blindness to the strangeness of her own position. But such shiftings and turnings and dichotomies and inconsistencies are part of the history of Ireland in these years. The period between the fall of Parnell and the end of the Civil War saw a great vacuum in Ireland which many opposing forces sought to fill. None of these forces — from the unionists in the north to Patrick Pearse and his followers in the south to the trade union movement to the landed gentry — remained stable. In the period between 1890 and 1925 every force changed and adapted.

Like many others, including those with the benefit of greater hindsight, both Yeats and Lady Gregory misread the period after the fall of Parnell. In "Ireland After Parnell", published in *The Trembling of the Veil* in 1922, Yeats wrote of "an intellectual movement at the first lull in politics … the sudden certainty that Ireland was to be like soft wax for years to come". "After Parnell," Lady Gregory wrote in 1911, "young men were no longer tied up in leagues and politics, their imagination called out for something more." Yet any study of the committee of the Gaelic League or the Gaelic Athletic Association in any town in Ireland in these years makes clear that a good number of the young men would quickly emerge as more interested in politics, and indeed revolution, than in culture or sport. The soft wax quietly hardened, and this process was both helped and hindered in ways both knowing and unwitting by Yeats and Lady Gregory and their associates.

At Coole in the summer of 1901, a year after she had determined to keep out of politics, Yeats told Lady Gregory of a dream "almost as distinct as a vision, of a cottage where there was well-being and firelight and talk of a marriage, and into the midst of that cottage there came an old woman in a long cloak" who was "Ireland herself, that Cathleen ni Houlihan for whom so many songs have been sung, and about whom so many stories have been told and for whose sake so many have gone to their death". This woman would lead the young man of the house away from domestic happiness to join the French who had landed at Killala.

It is now absolutely clear that the play that this dream became, *Cathleen Ni Houlihan*, though credited to Yeats, was written largely by Lady Gregory. The idea belonged to Yeats and Yeats wrote the chant of the old woman at the end. But he could not write peasant dialogue, and the play depends on the naturalistic setting, the talk of money and marriage, the sense of ease in family life in a smallholding. In the manuscript held in the Berg Collection in the New York Public Library, Lady Gregory has written in pencil on the first section of ten pages "All this mine alone", and "This with WBY" at the beginning of the second section. James Pethica has described how Lady Gregory managed in the play to temper Yeats's tendency "'to symbolise rather than to represent life' and grounded the development of the play within a realistic framework. Her emphasis on the emotional ties and hopes and dreams of the peasant family also invested Yeats's political allegory with tragic force, by vividly realizing the well-being that Cathleen's call destroys."

In her journal for 1922, Lady Gregory said that she wrote "all but all" of *Cathleen Ni Houlihan*. Lennox Robinson stated that "the verses in it are the poet's, but all the homely dialogue is Lady Gregory's. Indeed Yeats has told me more than once that the authorship of the play should be ascribed to her." Willie Fay also reported that Lady Gregory had written all the play "except the part of Cathleen".

It is clear that Lady Gregory contributed "directly and abundantly", in James Pethica's phrase, to Yeats's work for the theatre, especially to *On Baile's Strand*, *The Pot of Broth*, *The King's Threshold* and *Deirdre*. In his dedication of *Where There Is Nothing* to Lady Gregory in 1902, Yeats wrote: "I never did anything that went so easily and quickly, for when I hesitated, you had the right thought ready, and it was always you who gave the right turn to the phrase and gave it the ring of daily life. We finished several plays, of which this is the longest, in so few weeks, that if I were to say how few, I do not think anybody would believe me."

Although Yeats gave Lady Gregory some public credit for this collaboration, he never acknowledged the extent of her work on *Cathleen Ni Houlihan*. In a diary entry in 1925

Lady Gregory complained that his failure to credit her as co-author was "rather hard on me". Elizabeth Coxhead, in her literary portrait of Lady Gregory, wrote that "when her family ... urged her to stake her claim, she always refused with a smile, saying that she could not take from [Yeats] any part of what had proved, after all, his one real popular success".

The play was performed with George Russell's play *Deirdre* in Dublin in April 1902, with Maud Gonne playing Cathleen. Lady Gregory, according to Roy Foster, attended one rehearsal and "slipped away to Venice well before the first night". Yeats, in an interview with the *United Irishman*, said that his subject was "Ireland and its struggle for independence". "Apparently," Roy Foster wrote, "neither of them anticipated the response to their joint production." The hall was packed every night, and the effect of the play was powerful. It was short and stark, with no sub-plots or stylized dialogue until Cathleen herself appeared, and its message was clear: that young men would have to give up everything for Ireland. The audience and the ordinary people on the stage were as one, and both were visited by this haunting force, a woman both old and young, who would pull them towards heroism and away from everyday materialism. The critic Stephen Gwynn attended the performance and wrote: "I went home asking myself if such plays should be produced unless one was prepared for people to

go out to shoot and be shot … Yeats was not alone
responsible; no doubt but Lady Gregory helped him to get
the peasant speech so perfect; but above all Miss Gonne's
impersonation had stirred the audience as I have never seen
another audience stirred … Yeats has said somewhere that
his defect as a dramatist is that normal men do not interest him; but here in one brief theme he had expressed what
a hundred others have tried to do, the very spirit of a race
forever defeated and for ever insurgent against defeat. He
had linked this expression with a perfectly normal household group."

George Bernard Shaw later said that it was a play
"which might lead a man to do something foolish". By
1904, Yeats was ready to deny that "it was a political play
of a propaganda kind", but he was not convincing. Many
years later, he would wonder "Did that play of mine send
out / Certain men the English shot?".

It can be argued that one of the main reasons why
Lady Gregory did not want to claim co-authorship was her
own ambiguous relationship with this material: she kept
her friends in England, she remained a landlord, she did
not wish to be connected directly with the emotional call
for action that *Cathleen Ni Houlihan* and indeed Maud
Gonne proposed. But her own restraint, once she was away
from Coole and her role as a landlord, was always open to
other forces. She wanted and generally managed both to be

landlord and also to write stirringly about rebellion, although she made sure that her rebels' political ambitions were vague. Fortunately, her rebels never wanted land. Two other one-act plays to which she gave her name as author, *Gaol Gate* and *The Rising of the Moon*, both produced and published over the next few years, made no bones about her support for rebellion. Lennox Robinson wrote that *Cathleen Ni Houlihan* and *The Rising of the Moon* "made more rebels in Ireland than a thousand political speeches or a hundred reasoned books".

How she managed her two separate worlds in these years is a mystery, but she managed superbly. In these same years, she could write Yeats a description of a dance at Coole: "Our dance last night went off splendidly, lasted till three o'clock this morning, I wished you could have been there it was such a pretty bright sight, the drawing room cleared and lighted by close of fifty wax candles, the supper served on the twenty silver dishes, all the table silver and flowers and tempting dishes ... We were about thirty, chiefly cousins of Robert's and also two or three officers and a sister of Lord Westmeath's, Lady Emily Nugent ... It was the merriest dance I ever saw (my experience has not been great, Buckingham Palace and Indian Viceregal and Embassy Balls chiefly) ... Tomorrow I am giving a tea party to the old women in the workhouse."

Lady Gregory continued her friendship with Lady

Layard, whom she had known since the early days of her marriage. She stayed with her in London and in Venice. In May 1909 she wrote to Yeats from Venice: "The Royal Yacht is anchored off the Piazza and yesterday the Queen, the Empress of Russia and the Princess Victoria came to lunch here and were pleased and pleasant. There was a Russian Prince between me and your friend the Queen but she talked to me sometimes across him. I think she looks younger than ever. The Empress looks like a Phil May housemaid."

In *Cathleen Ni Houlihan*, *The Rising of the Moon* and *Gaol Gate*, indeed in the story of Cuchulain himself, the lone male hero was ready to sacrifice himself. He was an idealistic, inspirational figure, free from the mire of Land League politics. In *Cathleen Ni Houlihan*, the family's desire for more land is something the son will have no truck with now that the old woman has come to the house and the French have landed at Killala. There was no grubby land-hunger in the rhetoric of these heroes.

Thus it was easier for Lady Gregory to apply the same zeal to collecting her folklore as to collecting her rents. In her references to the tea party for the old women of the workhouse and to "your friend the Queen", there is a sense of the irony that her strange allegiances allowed her. She was also, on at least one occasion, frightened enough by what she herself had created to write to Frank Fay in 1907:

"I particularly didn't wish to have 'Gaol Gate' [in Galway] in the present state of agrarian excitement, it [might] be looked on as a direct incitement to crime."

Her plays could incite crime; but when crime came close to her, it kept her awake. There was no irony in her letter to Yeats in May 1912 about her tenants: "Dear Willie, I am in great trouble this week – my brother wrote last week that he had had a meeting with the tenants but that they could not come to terms at present. Then Monday was rent day and he wired 'Tenants demand 6/- in the pound reduction – no rents paid." This was a shock and gave me a sleepless night and in the morning I had a letter from him saying the tenants are trying to blackmail us – and that he is making preparations to seize their cattle end of this week or beginning of next, which will he thinks bring them to reason, especially as the bulk of them are really anxious to pay – I wrote to Father Fahy to do what he could, but this morning I decided to go home this afternoon, though Frank had told me not to come, as the cattle will be impounded in Coole, and I would be nervous – But I must do what I can to keep peace – I don't know what outside pressure has been brought to bear on them, for they had paid full rent up to this, and this is not a bad year – My terror is that if their cattle are seized they may retaliate and that could give Robert a turn against them for ever. It is a great shock and sorrow. Don't say anything about it." She wrote to her son that their agent "was sure that the seizures would bring them to their senses … He had arranged to start from Gort at 7 o'clock Friday morning, with eight Gort men, four Coole men and twenty police; to begin with the stock of the small tenants, and to sweep that of the larger ones as well."

The cattle raid in Coole did not take place, however, as a settlement was negotiated, Lady Gregory and Fr Fahy working as intermediaries. Robert, who was away, owned the estate and the rents were his income. "I hope you think I have done right," she wrote to him, "I have done what I think best for your happiness." This is the key to understand her role as landlord at Coole. The cold, ruthless tone in her letters to Yeats and Robert about the tenants was not because she was a landlord's daughter who could not shake off this tone. She held Coole for Robert. It was his heritage and his inheritance. No matter how she changed in other areas, she remained steadfast in this. It was her duty and she believed in doing her duty more than anything. She merely invented other duties, and when these seemed to conflict with her primary duty, her tone grew steely.

In 1910, in *The Green Helmet and Other Poems*, Yeats wrote twelve lines about Lady Gregory's plight as a landlord. The poem made no apology; it was Yeats at his most lofty. It was called "Upon a House Shaken by the Land Agitation":

How should the world be luckier if this house,
Where passion and precision have been one
Time out of mind, became too ruinous
To breed the lidless eye that loves the sun?
And the sweet laughing eagle thoughts that grow
Where wings have memory of wings, and all
That comes of the best knit to the best? [...]

Lady Gregory's mixture of high ideals and natural haughtiness gave her an inflexibility and sturdy determination that were invaluable when dealing with those who opposed her. Her gifts to govern men, her passion and precision, as Yeats put it, came into their own in the early years of the twentieth century when she became involved with the Abbey Theatre. She won her battles, partly because she kept her eye fiercely on her primary aim: to create a theatre that would add dignity to Ireland.

Her first battle was with Miss Horniman, the tea-heiress from Manchester who bankrolled the theatre in its early days and made great demands on the management and fellow directors while also making a pitch for the affections of W.B. Yeats. In many letters to Yeats, Lady Gregory deplored Miss Horniman's "vulgar arrogance and bullying" and suggested that she "should be locked up". She also called her "cracked", "a blood sucker", "a crocodile", "the Saxon shilling", "wicked", "a mad woman", "insane" and "a raving lunatic". If this was not enough to dislodge her, Lady Gregory pulled rank. "I have never treated her as an equal", she wrote to Yeats, "without regretting it." And later: "I think it is a mistake treating tradespeople as if they had one's own table of values."

Miss Horniman took particular exception to the Abbey's remaining open on the death of Edward VII in 1910. Lady Gregory was at Coole when she received the news of the king's death from Lennox Robinson. Her telegram — "should close through courtesy" — did not arrive in time for the matinee, and Robinson, whose decision-making processes were a constant scourge to Lady Gregory, decided that since the matinee had taken place, the evening performance should go on as well. Miss Horniman was opposed to the use of the theatre for political purposes and saw the non-closure as a political act; she sent many angry messages and threatened as usual to withdraw her subsidy. When it was suggested that Lady Gregory might have sent her telegram as a way of placating Miss Horniman, Lady Gregory grew very dignified and grand. She was no longer "the woman of the house that has to be minding the place, and listening to complaints and dividing her share of food". "My impulse was to close," she wrote, "but I thought I might be prejudiced by the fact of the King having been a personal friend of my husband, who had been his host and his guest and had received presents from him and being made by him a member of the Marlborough Club. But certainly in the few minutes I took to decide and to write my answer 'should close through courtesy' the idea of Miss Horniman or any letter of hers did not come into my mind at all."

This hauteur and invective were accompanied over several years by Lady Gregory's slow and deliberate preparations to have Miss Horniman removed. While Miss Horniman ranted and raved, Lady Gregory never lost her nerve. By early 1911, she had succeeded.

The actors were easier. Lady Gregory was tireless in her efforts to keep them in their place. She had a barm brack made for them regularly in Gort. Maire Ní Shiubhlaigh, or Miss Walker as Lady Gregory called her, wrote that "it was a huge cart-wheel of a fruit cake, filled with the richest ingredients, made specially by her own bakers at Gort for the casts of any of her new plays. It was a huge affair of several pounds weight and usually took two to carry in. It must have been two feet in circumference, and fully eight inches in depth." Her brack became part of the folklore of the Abbey Theatre. Willie Fay, one of her leading actors, called it "the father and mother of a brack ... A single slice of one of those Gort barm bracks was as good as a meal." Brinsley MacNamara, however, took a dim view of the brack: "It came in time to be regarded in an unkindly and suspicious way as something that had a sort of feudal touch about it, the kind of thing that grand ladies sometimes supplied for high jinks in the servants' hall. So great lumps of it would remain untaken and be relegated to the scene dock for consumption by the stage hands."

Many of Lady Gregory's letters to Yeats and journal entries are made up of accounts of the firm grip she was keeping on the actors, her war against the antics of Miss Allgood or the petulance of Miss Walker, the absence or indeed the presence of Miss Magee, the demands of the Fay brothers or Vaughan, and other pieces of insubordination or demands for more money by Miss Drago, Miss O'Dougherty and Miss Malony. "I have very little hope of keeping Fay," she wrote to Yeats in 1907, "and would not keep him but on the understanding that we are employers and he employed ... I would certainly dismiss Vaughan but we must think what excuse is best – it might be best to say we are offended by his acting." She cast a cold eye on all newcomers. In February 1916 she wrote to Yeats that a new actress, "Mrs Cruise O'Brien, was as bad as could be, with no redeeming point, amateurish, clumsy and revolting in appearance".

What the actors and actresses throught of Lady Gregory in turn may be gleaned from the memoirs of Maire Ní Shiubhlaigh. Lady Gregory, she wrote, would come to

Dublin when a new play was to be read by the Abbey players. She would take rooms in a hotel, "entertaining lavishly during her stay". Lady Gregory "inisted on reading over selected pieces to us in her hotel drawing room", Maire Ní Shiubhlaigh remembered. "Her odd lisping voice had a peculiar effect on speeches, especially those of the poetic sort, and, later, the lilting lines of J.M. Synge, which suffered much through her pronunciation. I think she rather fancied herself as an actress ... But she was a pleasant if at times rather condescending person, who treated us all as children in need of special advice."

Lady Gregory's condescending manner, and her readiness to do battle, and her tough attitude towards opposition, made all the difference when the artistic integrity of the Abbey Theatre was under attack. The importance of Yeats's and Lady Gregory's collaboration at the Abbey was not so much that words of theirs sent out certain men the English shot, but that during the time when they ran the theatre a number of enduring masterpieces were produced, notably the plays of Synge and O'Casey, and also George Bernard Shaw's *The Shewing-up of Blanco Posnet*.

Both Yeats and Lady Gregory maintained their relationship to a peasant culture they had dreamed into being and at the same time made no effort to repudiate their own Anglo-Irish heritage. This gave them an enormous advantage in both Ireland and London: they were members of a ruling class who lost none of their edge or high manners or old friends while espousing a new politics and a new art in Ireland. They were independent and they did what they liked, subject to no peer-group or class pressure. It was the mixture of ambiguity and arrogance in their position which made them ready for the exemplary battles they were now to fight for artistic freedom in Ireland, the right to stage the plays of Synge, Shaw and O'Casey. They, and no one else, had the strength of will and the class confidence and the belief in their cause to do battle with the *Playboy* rioters, the Catholic Church, the Lord Lieutenant and, when the time came, the new Irish state.

Lady Gregory first saw John Millington Synge in 1898. "I first saw him", she later wrote, "in the North Island of Aran. I was staying there, gathering folklore talking to the people, and felt a real pang of indignation when I passed another outsider walking here and there, talking also to the people. I was jealous of not being alone on the island among the fishers and seaweed gatherers. I did not speak to the stranger nor was he inclined to speak to me. He also looked on me as an intruder." Lady Gregory was forty-six; Synge was twenty-seven. He was a middle-class Protestant and, in Roy Foster's phrase, "an apprentice bohemian". He, like Lady Gregory, had proselytizing

Protestantism in his background, his uncle having been the first Protestant missionary on the Aran Islands. Both he and Lady Gregory had mothers who were addicted to salvation. Yeats had already met him in Paris, and soon he was invited to Coole.

Synge was a great mystery: solitary, detached, overeducated, watchful. The exuberance and depth of feeling in his work were strangely absent from his personality. His sophistication, his irony and his wide reading responded warmly to the speech patterns, the way of life and the landscape he found in the west of Ireland. He had, Lady Gregory wrote, "done no good work until he came back to his own country. It was there that he found all he wanted, fable, emotion, style ... bringing a cultured mind to a mass of primitive material, putting clearer and lasting form to the clumsily expressed emotion of a whole countryside." Synge did not make his characters simple or charming or harmless, nor did he seek to stir up national feeling, unless uproarious laughter and wild paganism were forms of national feeling. Although he did not seem to have any special wish, in Lady Gregory's phrase, to add dignity to Ireland, he wrote with feeling and awe and tenderness about the "folk-imagination of these fine people" in rural Ireland. In his Preface to *The Playboy of the Western World* he wrote that "anyone who has lived in real intimacy with the Irish peasantry will know that the wildest sayings and ideas in the play are tame indeed, compared with the fancies one may hear in any hillside cabin in Geesala, or Carraroe, or Dingle Bay". Despite Synge's invocation of the people, it was clear that the young men who had crowded in to see *Cathleen Ni Houlihan*, growing slowly more militant and confident in the years that followed its production, were going to be greatly offended by Synge's plays.

The Shadow of the Glen, in which a woman runs away with a tramp, was first performed in 1903, and caused a deep rift between Yeats and Lady Gregory on one side and diehard nationalists – including Arthur Griffith, who founded Sinn Féin in that year – on the other. Griffith wrote that the play was "a story invented by the wits of decadent Greece and introduced, with amendments, into Latin literature by the most infamous of Roman writers, Petronius Arbiter, the pander of Nero ... Mr Synge's Nora Burke [who runs away with the tramp] is not an Irish Nora Burke, his play is not a work of genius – Irish or otherwise – it is a foul echo from degenerate Greece." Maud Gonne also joined the attack: "Mr Yeats asks for freedom for the theatre, freedom even from patriotic captivity. I would ask for freedom for it from one thing more deadly than all else – freedom from the insidious and destructive tyranny of foreign influence." Yeats's response to the attacks included an article called "The National Theatre and Three Sorts of Ignorance". The second sort of ignorance was, he wrote, "the more ignorant sort of priest, who forgetful of the great traditions of the Church, would deny all ideas that might perplex a parish of farmers or artisans or half-educated shopkeepers". This was published in the *United Irishman*. "For a liberal Protestant to refer to Catholicism this way in public", Roy Foster wrote, "broke one of the taboos which sustained the uneasy collusions of Irish life; if to some his stance seemed self-regarding and amoral, to others his language smacked of the Protestant Ascendancy at its most contemptuous."

Yeats's third sort of ignorance was that of "the politicians, and not always of the most ignorant sort, who would reject every idea which is not of immediate service to his cause". Towards the end of 1906, all three sorts of ignorance heard a rumour that there was a new Synge play in closed rehearsal at the Abbey Theatre which was likely to be even more offensive than *The Shadow of the Glen*.

What remains fascinating about the riots and controversies surrounding *The Playboy of the Western World* is how, once under pressure, the founders of the Abbey Theatre reverted to their Ascendancy and Protestant backgrounds. It was as though they forgot the transformation they had made in themselves, and behaved like a reformed alcoholic on a short spree. The old Fenian John O'Leary had warned Yeats that in Ireland you must have either the Fenians or the Church on your side. In writing *The Countess*

Cathleen, his first play, he had alienated elements in the Church; in staging *The Shadow of the Glen* he had alienated elements in the Fenians. Now, in one fell swoop, he had alienated both.

After a week of riots in the theatre, there was, on Yeats's suggestion, a public debate held in the Abbey on 4 February. Synge was too ill and uninterested to attend; Lady Gregory remained in the background. Yeats took the stage. Referring to a priest in Liverpool who had withdrawn a play because of the public's objection, Yeats said of the Abbey directors: "we have not such pliant bones and did not learn in the houses that bred us a suppliant knee". The audience would have understood this very clearly as a statement of arrogant Ascendancy values over suppliant Roman ones. When Yeats's father in the same debate referred to Ireland as an island of saints and scholars and then, sneeringly, referred to "plaster saints" ("his beautiful mischievous head thrown back", as Yeats described him many years later in "Beautiful Lofty Things"), the audience would also have understood his remark as an insult to Catholicism. ("Get the loy," someone shouted to Yeats as his father spoke.) Lady Gregory's nephew led a group of Trinity students to the theatre to defend the play and offer what was perhaps most notably absent in the debate – a rendering of "God Save the King". And as the disturbances continued in the theatre, the Abbey directors, as property-owners, knew what to do: they called the police, who arrested rioters. The calling of the police did not win them many friends in nationalist Ireland.

Yeats, for the public debate, sat on the stage, wearing his bow tie, wallowing in all his beautiful ambiguity. He had called the police and he could also declare, in case anyone wished to question his patriotic credentials, that he spoke as the author of *Cathleen Ni Houlihan*. Joseph Holloway, who kept a diary of Dublin theatre life, wrote: "The odd thing is that Fay told me Lady Gregory wrote the whole of it except the part of 'Cathleen'."

Lady Gregory disliked *The Playboy of the Western World*; both she and Yeats had already removed words and phrases from the acting text. There would always be tension between Lady Gregory and Synge. Although he told her that her translation of Cuchulain was part of his daily bread, Synge felt, with some reason, that Lady Gregory promoted Yeats's work for the theatre and, indeed, her own work over his, which he rightly felt was superior. She, in turn, liked him as little as his play. After his death, there is a crossed-out passage in the manuscript of her journals where she wrote: "One doesn't want a series of panegyrics and we can't say, don't want to say what was true, he was ungracious to his fellow workers, authors and actors, ready in accepting praise, grudging in giving it ... On tour he thought of his own play only, gave no help to ours and if he repeated compliments they were to his own." Yeats in his journal wrote of Synge's "complete absorption in his own dream. I never heard him praise any writer, living or dead, but some old French farce-writer."

After his death, Lady Gregory wrote to Yeats: "You did more than anyone for him, you gave him his means of expression. You have given me mine, but I should have found something else to do, though not anything coming near this, but I don't think Synge would have done anything but drift but for you and the theatre." And also: "I think you and I supplied him with vitality when he was with us as the wild people did in the Blaskets."

Lady Gregory had remarked some years earlier that "we are all born bigots in Ireland". Yeats in his journal for 1914 remarked: "A long continuity of culture like that at Coole could not have arisen and never has arisen, in a single Catholic family in Ireland since the Middle Ages." Unlike the Yeatses, however, Lady Gregory confined her anti-Catholicism to a number of jokes and sharp, funny comments in her letters and journals. In February 1888, for example, she found dinner at the Denbighs' "rather dull, all Catholics or perverts, except Lady Louisa Legge". In Rome, she saw the Pope and thought the afternoon wasted, "unless it is a gain to feel more indignantly Protestant than ever". In 1899 she wrote to Yeats about her Catholic neighbour Edward Martyn: "These papists haven't the courage of a mouse." In 1909, two years after *The Playboy*, she acidly placed the conflict between the Abbey directors and the Catholic nationalist mob in starker and, indeed, funnier terms: "It is the old battle," she wrote to Yeats, "between those who use a toothbrush and those who don't."

As Catholic, nationalist and cavity-ridden Ireland felt more indignantly against *The Playboy of the Western World*, Lady Gregory needed all her courage. She and Yeats had to withdraw the play from performance in Birmingham during the English tour and then justify this to an irate Synge. And she had to go back to Coole, where because of her involvement with Synge's play she was forbidden by the local council to visit the workhouse or entertain the schoolchildren in Gort. When she asked Fr Fahy to intercede for her, he replied: "The request coming from you shall have all the more weight when forwarded to the board by yourself." The people without toothbrushes were getting their revenge.

Between 16 February and 8 March 1909 George Bernard Shaw wrote his own version of *The Playboy*; it was a short play called *The Shewing-up of Blanco Posnet: A Sermon in Crude Melodrama*, and it was set in America, Blanco being an unrepentant horse thief with strong views on the Almighty.

There were also several foul-mouthed women, and a lot of very funny, sometimes silly and often irreverent and blaspheming dialogue. Like *The Playboy*, it was deeply objectionable as much in its general tone as in its particulars. Shaw offered it to the actor Beerbohm Tree, who was to get a knighthood within three months. Tree's concerns about the blasphemy and general immorality in the play were irrelevant because the Lord Chamberlain was prepared to ban the play. The Chamberlain's remit did not extend to Dublin, however, and when Shaw handed the script to Lady Gregory, she took it to Yeats and they decided to produce it at the Abbey.

This would prove, if anyone needed proof (and indeed some did), that the Abbey Theatre would oppose censorship from every quarter. Yeats and Lady Gregory had stood up to the rabble; now they would, with the same hauteur and moral authority, stand up to Dublin Castle. In August 1909 Lady Gregory herself directed the play while Yeats stayed at Coole; it was the first play she had directed alone. Soon, the authorities wrote to her: "The play does not deal with an Irish subject, and it is not an Irish play in any other sense than that its author was born in Ireland. It is now proposed to produce this play in the Abbey Theatre which was founded for the express purpose of encouraging dramatic art in Ireland and of fostering a dramatic school growing out of the life of the country." It was pointed out that the fact that the censor's remit did not extend to Dublin was "an accidental freedom". Lady Gregory was warned that the theatre could lose its patent.

In *Our Irish Theatre*, Lady Gregory described with great relish the meetings she had with the authorities. She must have enjoyed telling James Dougherty, the Under-Secretary, that "the subject of the play is a man, a horse-thief, shaking his fist at Heaven, and finding afterwards that Heaven is too strong for him. If there were no defiance, there could be no victory. It is the same theme that Milton has taken in Satan's defiance in Paradise Lost." At a further meeting which Yeats attended, Dougherty "implored us ... to save the Lord Lieutenant from his delicate position". "Can you suggest no way out?" he asked. "None, except our being left alone," they told him. "Oh Lady Gregory," he said, "appeal to your own common sense." Both Dougherty and the Lord Lieutenant himself, Lord Aberdeen, were interested in drama and also in favour of Home Rule. They were a symptom of England's weakening hold on Ireland. They were easy pickings.

Shaw wrote opposing a private performance: "Threaten that we shall be suppressed; that we shall be made martyrs of; that we shall suffer as much and as publicly as possible. Tell them that they can depend on me to burn with a brighter blaze than all Foxe's martyrs." Finally, when the Castle threatened to forbid the performance of the play,

Yeats and Lady Gregory, realizing what was at stake – they would lose their patent and be fined – "very sadly … agreed that we must give up the fight. We did not say a word of this at the Abbey but went on rehearsing as usual."

It is difficult to imagine them making a decision to give up the fight, who had never given one up before. It makes for a better story, however, especially one with such a triumphant ending. "When we had left the Theatre," Lady Gregory wrote, "and were walking through the lamp-lighted streets, we found that during those two or three hours our minds had come to the same decision, that we had given our word, that at all risks we must keep it or it would never be trusted again; that we must in no case go back, but must go on at any cost." Dublin Castle caved in and the play opened, to capacity audiences and huge publicity, on 25 August. Yeats issued a statement: "Tomorrow night Blanco Posnet will have a triumph. The audience will look at one another in amazement, asking what on earth did the English Censor discover objectionable. They will understand instantly. The root of the whole difference between us and England in such matters is that though there might be some truth in the old charge that we are not truthful to one another here in Ireland, we are certainly always true to ourselves. In England they have learned from commerce to be truthful to one another, but they are great liars when alone."

Even Patrick Pearse was impressed, praising Yeats and Lady Gregory for "making a fight for Irish freedom from an English censorship". In her account of the opening night, Lady Gregory reported that "a stranger outside asked what was going on in the Theatre. 'They are defying the Lord Lieutenant,' was the answer; and when the crowd heard the cheering, they took it up and it went far out through the streets." George Bernard Shaw later said that Lady Gregory was "the greatest living Irishwoman". However, her daughter-in-law Margaret, recently married to Robert, told Lady Dunsany that, although Yeats had not seen any rehearsals, "realizing that all the English and foreign critics had collected and that there was a stir, he asked her to let him take the [last dress] rehearsal, saying he wished the reporters to think he had stage managed it, and she is so used to giving way to him that she agreed".

Among the audience that night was the twenty-seven-year-old James Joyce, home briefly from Trieste, and he published an account of the whole business in *Il Piccolo della Sera* in Trieste. "Dubliners," he wrote, "who care nothing for art, but love an argument passionately, rubbed their hands with joy ... and the little theatre was so filled at the first performance that it literally sold out more than seven times over ... at the curtain fall, a thunderous applause summoned the actors for repeated curtain calls." For Joyce, the play confirmed his views on Shaw. "Nothing more flimsy can be imagined, and the playgoer asks himself in wonder why on earth the play was interdicted by the censor. Shaw is a born preacher. His lively and talkative spirit cannot stand to be subjected to the noble and bare style appropriate to modern playwriting ... In this case he has dug up the central incident of his *Devil's Disciple* and transformed it into a sermon. The transformation is too abrupt to be convincing as a sermon, and the art is too poor to make it convincing as drama."

Joyce had known Lady Gregory since 1902. He had read his poems to her and asked for advice. She invited him to Coole, but he did not go, deciding instead to go to Paris. He wrote to her: "I am going alone and friendless ... into another country ... I do not know what will happen to me in Paris but my case can hardly be worse than it is here ... And though I seem to have been driven out of my country here as a misbeliever I have found no man yet with a faith like mine." Lady Gregory wrote to Yeats: "I am afraid he will knock his ribs against the earth, but he has grit and will succeed in the end. You should write and ask him to breakfast with you on the morning he arrives, if you can get up early enough, and feed him and take care of him and give him dinner at Victoria before he goes and help him on his way. I am writing to various people who might possibly get him tuition, and to Synge who could at least tell him of cheap lodgings." Yeats did as he was told. Arriving at Euston Station at six in the morning to meet Joyce, he took the young writer around to meet people he thought might be useful to him, finding him "unexpectedly amiable".

Joyce's amiability took a sudden turn for the worse soon after he arrived in Paris. In December 1902 he wrote to Lady Gregory, telling her that "to create poetry out of French life is impossible". In March 1903 he was asked by the literary editor of the *Daily Express* in Dublin, to whom Lady Gregory had introduced him, to review her *Poets and Dreamers*. Despite his intermittent use of a toothbrush, his teeth were sharp enough to bite the hand. In her book, he wrote, Lady Gregory "has explored in a land almost fabulous in its sorrow and senility". The storyteller from whom Lady Gregory took the stories had a mind, he wrote, "feeble and sleepy ... He begins one story and wanders from it into another story, and none of the stories has any satisfying imaginative wholeness ... In fine, her book, wherever it treats of the 'folk', sets forth in the fullness of its senility a class of mind which Mr Yeats has set forth with such delicate skepticism in his happiest book *The Celtic Twilight.*"

On the same day as the review appeared, Synge reported to Lady Gregory from Paris that Joyce was "being won over by the charm of French life" while remaining penniless and indolent. "I cannot think he will ever be a poet of importance," Synge wrote, "but his intellect is extraordinarily keen and if he keeps fairly sane he ought to do excellent essay-writing." Later that same year, as his mother was dying, Joyce came back to Dublin and crashed a party at Lady Gregory's; a fellow guest watched him "with his air of half-timid effrontery, advancing towards his unwilling hostess and turning away from her to watch the crowd". A year later, as he was getting ready once more to leave Ireland, he managed to touch Lady Gregory for five pounds. Her reward was to be one of Yeats's "giddy dames" in his broadside "The Holy Office", which he had the good sense not to send to her when he published it in Pola in 1905. The following year he wrote to his brother to say that "W.B. Yeats ought to marry Lady Gregory – to kill talk", and in "Gas from a Burner" in 1912 he referred to her as "Gregory of the Golden Mouth". Twenty years later, just after the publication of *Ulysses*, he wrote her a very rude letter in reply to her request for permission to quote from a letter of his: "While thanking you for the friendly remembrance contained in it, and for acts of kindness in the past, I shall feel very much obliged if you will omit from your forthcoming book, which I understand is largely a history of the Irish literary movement, all letters of mine and all mention of me. In doing so you will be acting in strict accordance with the spirit of that movement, inasmuch as since the date of my letter, twenty years ago, no mention of me or of my struggles or of my writings has been made publicly by any person connected with it ... May I ask you to be kind enough to convey to Mr Yeats, for whose writing I have always had the greatest admiration, my thanks for his favourable opinion [of *Ulysses*], which I value very highly."

It would be easy to read this as an example of an arrogant young genius becoming a middle-aged curmudgeon, but it discloses something more interesting and revealing. Once her Cuchulain translation was in print and the Abbey Theatre established, Lady Gregory held power in Ireland. Many young men and woman of talent followed her, writing peasant plays or acting in them, going west in search of knowledge and wisdom, believing in the uncomplicated tradition she had invented. The stories she wrote were simple, and her aim too was simple: to add dignity to Ireland, to revive the national spirit. The cultural nationalist movement was diverse: it contained Griffith and Pearse, whose vision and projects were rather more fierce than those of Yeats and Synge, whom it also contained. Lady Gregory would attempt to work with Pearse as much as with Synge. In a letter to Yeats in December 1904, around the same time as she gave Joyce five pounds, she wrote about her discussions with Pearse regarding an Irish-language theatre: "In answering Pearse I said I believed all those who were in earnest in wishing to develop the drama as part of our national life would be together again, and we on our side were very anxious to avoid hard or discourteous words and had made every possible concession, and that we had proposed some time ago that those who did not get on with us should take up the development of Gaelic Drama, in which they could work side by side with us and with our help. That is a little bait for him."

Joyce's relationship to Irish cultural nationalism remained complex. The very views that he himself put forward when he wrote for the Italian press, he mocked in *Ulysses*. In "The Dead", the very cosmopolitan self that Joyce was in the process of creating was dramatically and hauntingly undermined by the call of the west. He understood the immense power of what Lady Gregory was proposing. He made use of it in his work, but he knew that, if he gave in to it, it would destroy him. There was a whole world under Lady Gregory's nose — of clerks and servants and lower-middle-class Catholics and Dublin loungers and layabouts — which she never noticed. They belonged to city life. They were Irish, but not in the way she had redefined the meaning of being Irish. They had no interest in ancient stories, but much interest in backing horses. They knew Victorian ballads as much as rebel songs. Later, when Sean O'Casey appeared, she would have to consider this world, but by then she had consolidated her position.

Lady Gregory thought that Joyce's *A Portrait of the Artist as a Young Man* was "a model autobiography". In the last pages of the book, our hero keeps a diary. One of the last entries tells of John Alphonsus Mulrennan, who had just returned from the West of Ireland, from the world which Lady Gregory had made central in the Irish experience and from which Joyce sought to escape. "He told us he met a man there in a mountain cabin. Old man had red eyes and a short pipe. Old man spoke Irish. Mulrennan spoke Irish. Then old man and Mulrennan spoke English. Mulrennan spoke to him about universe and stars. Old man sat, listened, smoked, spat. Then said: —Ah, there must be terrible queer creatures at the latter end of the world.

"I fear him. I fear his red-rimmed horny eyes. It is with him I must struggle all through this night till days come, till he or I lie dead ..."

In 1911, in the United States, elements in the Church and the Fenians were waiting for the Abbey Theatre to arrive with *The Playboy of the Western World*, which, they had heard, mocked the purity of Irish women, a matter very close to their hearts. Lady Gregory sailed to the United States in September of that year. She had planned to spend a "quiet winter, writing and planting trees" and waiting for the birth of her second grandchild. (Her first, Richard, had been born in 1909.) Instead, because Yeats asked her to go with the Abbey Players, she had the richest and most rewarding and most exciting months of her life, almost a mirror image of her time in Egypt thirty years earlier when she combined foreign travel, a great political cause and a secret passion.

John Quinn was forty-one; Lady Gregory was fifty-nine. He was a rich and brilliant New York lawyer, art collector and connoisseur, with, in Roy Foster's phrase, "an eye for the first-rate". On a visit to Ireland in 1902, he had travelled west with Jack B. Yeats and attended the unveiling of the new tomb for Raftery, the blind poet, which Lady Gregory had erected. Afterwards, he joined her and Yeats and Douglas Hyde and others at Coole, being astounded not only by the lush surroundings but also by the seriousness and intensity and talent of his fellow house guests. "These were wonderful nights," he wrote, "long nights filled with good talk." He corresponded with the Yeats family and Lady Gregory over many years, offering assistance both moral and practical. When Yeats's father moved to New York in December 1907, complete with his considerable wit and indolence, and then refused to come home – he died there in 1922 – he was bankrolled and cared for by John Quinn. The old man said that Quinn was "the nearest approach to an angel in my experience".

As soon as she arrived in the United States, Lady Gregory was treated as a celebrity. Her being a "Lady" made her interesting to start with, but she was a lady with a controversial Irish play in tow. Journalists followed her everywhere she went, copiously misquoting her. ("When I say pig, it comes out sausage," she wrote to Robert.) The hostesses of the day lionized her. ("Mrs Jack Gardner, who is the leader of fashion [in Boston], and has a large collection of pictures, came and seized my hands and said 'you are a darling, a darling, a darling'.")

Boston was easy, despite some protests and complaints; so too Providence, where the Police Commissioners "found nothing to object to in the play but enjoyed every minute of it". She didn't think much of Washington. (She wrote to Yeats: "There doesn't seem to be much population, except members of government and niggers.") In Washington she was invited to the White House and met President Taft. ("When I was standing near him talking, something soft and pillowy touched me, it was his tummy which is the size of Sancho Panza's.")

Lady Gregory had taken no part in the public debate about *The Playboy* at the Abbey; unlike Yeats, she had no experience of speaking in public. Now, since there was huge demand for her to speak, she began to give lectures, and this newly discovered facility was another aspect of the great novelty of America. In November, as she arrived in New York and stayed at the Algonquin Hotel, the priests began to preach against *The Playboy*. When the disturbances in the theatre began, as Quinn had warned her they would, she went backstage and "knelt in the opening of the hearth, calling to every actor who came within earshot that they must not stop for a moment". It amused her that the protesters threw both rosaries and stinkpots.

Former president Teddy Roosevelt, who had admired her Cuchulain translation, sat in the same box in the theatre as Lady Gregory and spoke afterwards about his admiration for the play. "When we got to the theatre," she wrote, "and into the box, people saw Roosevelt and began to clap and at last he had to get up, and he took my hand and dragged me on my feet too and there was renewed clapping."

Lady Gregory spent day and night being fêted and interviewed; the rest of the time she wrote letters home. She kept copies of these letters and used them as the basis for a chapter of her book *Our Irish Theatre*, which appeared in 1913, but the chapter lacks the astonishing vitality of the letters, especially those to her son Robert. Her indignation and malice and indiscretion are matched by sheer delight at her adventures and an eye for absurdity and detail and a sense of wonder that this was happening to her. "I have nice rooms now," she wrote to him, "on the ninth floor, there are twenty-two floors altogether, the place riddled with telephones and radiators etc and I was glad to hear the voice of a fat housemaid from Mayo a while ago. It is a strange fate that sends me into battle after my peaceable life for so many years and especially over Playboy that I have never really loved, but one has to carry through one's job."

The real trouble came in Philadelphia, where the cast was arrested. Lady Gregory called John Quinn and told him that she "would sooner go to her death than give in", adding in a letter to her son that she "should like to avoid arrest because of the publicity, one would feel like a suffragette". Quinn had been watching the coverage of *The Playboy* very carefully. He wrote to her: "The policemen that ought to be put in the theater ought to be Irish policemen; then the town would have the edifying spectacle of Irish policemen ejecting Irish rowdies from an Irish play. I have not seen anything like the bitterness or unfairness of these attacks both by Irish ignoramuses and abnormal churchmen since the last days of Parnell."

Once the players had been arrested, Quinn took over the legal case and caused enormous excitement by arriving in the courtroom, fresh from New York, just in time to cross-examine a witness and make "a very fine speech". The actors, she wrote, "adore John Quinn, and his name will pass into folk-lore like those stories of O'Connell suddenly appearing at trials. He spoke splendidly, with fire and full knowledge." In her book, Lady Gregory watered down her great hatred for the other side, the Irish-Americans without toothbrushes, which she expressed in her letters to Robert: "The witnesses brought against us were the most villainous-looking creatures. I wanted to get a snap-

shooter but could not get through the crowds. Their faces would have been enough to exonerate us." She also left out what she told Robert on Christmas Day 1911: "Quinn has given me a very small and simple gold watch bracelet, I like it, though it doesn't look the 180 dollars I saw on the ticket when I tried it on! ... Quinn won't go bankrupt at present over it, as yesterday he was kept all day on unexpected business and came in at 10.30 to explain it was a reconstruction of a railway company he had been suddenly asked to undertake and his fee will be 10,000 pounds in shares."

When the tour was over, Lady Gregory stayed with John Quinn for almost a week. The letters she wrote to him on her return to Ireland in March 1912, when she celebrated her sixtieth birthday, and in April, suggest the intensity of their relationship during that short time. "My dear John," she wrote, "I think you are never out of my mind – though sometimes all seems a dream, a wonderful dream ... How good you were to me! How happy I was with you. How much I love you!"; and "My John, my dear John, my own John, not other people's John, I love you, I care for you, I know you, I want you, I believe in you, I see you always"; and "Oh my darling, am I now lonely after you? Do I not awake looking for you ... Why do I love you so much? ... It is some call that came in a moment – something impetuous and masterful about you that satisfies me."

Quinn's letters to her, which he kept copies of, are in the New York Public Library alongside her letters to him, including the letters quoted above. He was a rambling, deeply opinionated, gossipy correspondent. The fact that he dictated many of the letters gave him ample opportunity to be long-winded, but it also meant that he was careful. "I often think of you over there with the two grandchildren," he wrote in November 1913, "and your work and your success and the full rich life you lead." And three years later: "What a wonderful woman you are, with the energy of a Roosevelt and more balance! If you had been in Redmond's place there would have been home rule long ago." And two years after that: "I have always said that you were the most wonderful woman I have ever met."

While these admiring letters from Quinn lack the intimate, ardent tone of Lady Gregory's letters to him from 1912 and tell us nothing more about the nature of their relationship, it is clear there some of his letters are missing. Thirty years earlier, Lady Gregory had destroyed the sonnets she wrote to Wilfrid Scawen Blunt, sending him the poems in disguised handwriting but keeping no copies; now, at Coole, she told John Quinn: "your dear letter goes into the fire tonight. I must keep it till then."

Between her husband's death in 1892 and Robert's coming of age ten years later, Lady Gregory worked to clear the debts on the estate. From 1902, Robert was the owner of the house and the estate, although she had a right, according to Sir William's will, to live in the house for her lifetime. There was an intermittent conflict between Robert's interest in being master in his own house, seated at the head of his own table, and his mother's interest in having Yeats at the head of the table, offering him the master bedroom and devoting her household to the cause of the poet's comfort.

Sir Ian Hamilton, a cousin of Lady Gregory's, described Yeats at Coole: "No one even can have heard anyone play up to him like Lady Gregory ... All along the passage for some distance on either side of Yeats's door were laid thick rugs to prevent the slightest sound reaching the holy of holies – Yeats's bed. Down the passage every now and then would tiptoe a maid with a tray ... All suggestions that I could cheer him up a good deal if I went into his room and had a chat were met with horror."

Early in their friendship, Lady Gregory had written to Yeats: "I want you to have all you want, and I believe that suffering has done all it can for your soul, and that peace and happiness will be best for both soul and body now." A year later she wrote: "How bad of you to get ill just when I am not there to look after you! Do take care of yourself now, and feed yourself properly — and with any threatening of rheumatism you should look to your underwear."

In September 1907 Robert Gregory married Margaret Parry. Although the Gregorys lived much in London and Paris, Robert's resentment at Yeats's usurpation of his rightful place at Coole was exacerbated, if anything, by his marriage. In 1913 Lady Gregory wrote to Yeats: "I wonder if you would mind ordering some wine for yourself this time or is it dry sherry — and perhaps a special decanter. I will explain this strange request when we meet." In her biography of Lady Gregory, Mary Lou Kohfeldt wrote that "Robert Gregory was startled one evening when he called for a bottle of an especially fine vintage Torquey laid down by his father to find it was all gone, served bottle by bottle by his mother to Willie over the years." During the First World War, while Robert was in the British Army, Lady Gregory wrote to Yeats about the accounts at Coole, which she was about to go through with Margaret: "If as bad as I think and if you are well off in the summer, I'm afraid I must ask you to pay what will cover your food (not your lodging)."

Although he was a talented painter and stage designer, Robert did not have his mother's single-mindedness or energy. And it was clear that the days of landlords living on income from rents was coming to an end in Ireland. In 1909 Yeats wrote in his journal: "I thought of this house, slowly perfecting itself and the life within it in ever-increasing intensity of labour, and then of its probably sinking away through courteous incompetence, or rather sheer weakness of will, for ability has not failed in young Gregory." In 1912 Yeats wrote an eight-line poem called "The New Faces" about Coole, imagining its mistress dead and the new generation in control. In what Roy Foster calls "one of his moments of superb tactlessness", Yeats sent Lady Gregory the poem. She was about to return to New York with the Abbey to see John Quinn once more and it is unlikely that she was flattered by the poem or that she would have shown it with pride to the eponymous new faces, her son and daughter-in-law. She wrote to him: "The lines are very touching. I have often thought our ghosts will haunt that path and our talk hang in the air — It is good to have a meeting place anyhow, in this place where so many children of our minds were born. You won't publish it just now? — I think not." He did not publish it for ten years.

Her influence on him did not only include delaying publication to save her and her family from pain, but also in 1914 involved hurrying publication as a way of smiting her enemy. Her enemy, and the enemy of many others at that time including Yeats himself, was George Moore, who had published a new volume of memoirs. Moore had, as already noted, been forced to delete the passage in his first volume suggesting that Lady Gregory had in her youth attempted to convert Catholics to the Protestant religion. ("I think it is a good thing to have got the better of him," she wrote to Yeats.) Nonetheless, Lady Gregory told Yeats at the time that she "shook with laughter" at Moore's description of Edward Martyn. "No one ought ever to speak to him again, though I suppose we shall all do so," she added.

Now she was in a rage, and her nephew Hugh Lane was also in a rage. She wrote to Yeats, "I have (by request of Hugh Lane who has been thinking of an action – but don't mention this) been reading Moore's book – it is unspeakably filthy and insolent." The third volume of Moore's memoirs dwelt at great length on Yeats, Synge, Lady Gregory and Hugh Lane. The tone was garrulous and irreverent, and it is hard, even still, not to shake with laughter at some of his remarks, including those about Yeats ("lately returned to us from the States with a paunch, a huge stride, and an immense fur overcoat") attacking the middle classes thus causing Moore, who had inherited ten thousand acres, to ask himself "why our Willie Yeats should feel himself called upon to denounce his own class".

Moore had much to say about Synge, including: "Synge's death seems to have done him a great deal of good; he was not cold in his grave when his plays began to sell like hot cakes." He accused Lady Gregory of plagiarism in her Cuchulain translation and went on to describe her in tones that lacked the respect Lady Gregory normally commanded: "Lady Gregory has never been for me a real person. I imagine her without a mother, or father, or sisters, or brothers, sans attaché." He was not present, he wrote, for her first meeting with Yeats, "but from Edward [Martyn]'s account of the meeting she seems to have recognized her need in Yeats at once." Moore proceeded to patronize and mock her plays: "We must get it into our heads that the Abbey Theatre would have come to naught but for Lady Gregory's talent for rolling up little anecdotes into one-act plays." His remarks on Hugh Lane, who was possibly homosexual and certainly an advanced bachelor, were the most outrageous, as he described an afternoon when Lady Gregory "had occasion to go to her bedroom, and to her surprise found her wardrobe open and Hugh trying on her skirts before the glass".

Earlier, Lady Gregory had written to Yeats about Moore: "I didn't send my answer to Moore after all. I was afraid he might himself put a note in the English Review, which would probably be worse than the first offence – I wish you would publish that second poem as soon as possible, in some weekly paper, such as the Saturday or Nation, and put some title as 'suggested of a lately published article'. It is the best answer to give, and the simile of the dog would stick to him."

Eighteen days later, on 7 February 1914 Yeats published "Notoriety" in *The New Statesman*. It ended, "all my priceless things / Are but a post the passing dogs defile." The subtitle was "Suggested by a recent magazine article". Moore and his ten thousand acres had been briefly put in their place.

Lady Gregory was in Coole for Easter 1916. On 27 April, when the Rising was still going on in Dublin but no clear news had come to Coole except reports of local unrest (which she always viewed differently from national unrest), Lady Gregory wrote to Yeats: "It is terrible to think of the executions or killings that are sure to come – yet it must be so – we had been at the mercy of a rabble for a long time both here and in Dublin, with no apparent policy." On 7 May she wrote to Yeats: "I see in the paper today that MacBride has been executed – the best end that could come to him, giving him back dignity. And what a release for her! ... I am sorry for Pearce [*sic*] and McDonogh [*sic*], the only ones I knew among the leaders."

Slowly, however, her attitude changed. On 13 May she wrote to Yeats: "My mind is filled with sorrow at the Dublin tragedy, the death of Pearse and McDonogh, who ought to have been on our side, the side of intellectual freedom and I keep wondering whether we could have brought them into the intellectual movement. Perhaps these Abbey lectures we spoke of might have helped ... It seems as if the leaders were what is wanted in Ireland and will be even more wanted in the future – fearless and imaginative opposition to the conventional and opportunistic parliamentarians who have never helped our work even by intelligent opposition – Dillon just denounces us in his dull popular way." But fearless and imaginative leaders of the Rising were different from the local republicans in Galway to whom Lady Gregory refers in the same letter: "We have been calling out against those armed bullies who have been terrorizing the District for the last couple of years ... just village tyrants drifting about in search of trouble." The next day she wrote again to Yeats about the Abbey Theatre: "What I am rather upset by today is the putting on of Playboy at this moment – our management have shirked it for years and now it seems as if we were snatching a rather mean triumph in putting it forward just as those who might have attacked it are dead or in prison ... I believe we should have done it but for the Rising."

On 20 August 1916 Lady Gregory wrote a crucial letter to Yeats, who was staying with Maud Gonne in France and having much amorous discussion with her daughter Iseult, to say that she had been "a little puzzled" by his "apparent indifference to Ireland after your excitement after the Rising. I believe there is a great deal you can do, all is unrest and discontent — there is nowhere for the imagination to rest — but there must be some spiritual building possible, just as after Parnell's fall, but perhaps more intense, and you have a big name among the young men."

The following month Yeats wrote his poem "Easter 1916", whose listing of the names of the executed dead and whose refrain "A terrible beauty is born" had all the rhetoric of a nationalist ballad and offered a grandeur to what happened, giving a larger and more intense meaning to the "unrest and discontent" of Lady Gregory's letter. (Wilfrid Scawen Blunt at first believed that Lady Gregory had written the poem.) Later, the poem would be seen as a part of the great change in Irish politics which led to the Sinn Féin victory in the 1918 election and the death of the Irish Parliamentary Party. What's strange is that the poem was not published instantly in a periodical or a pamphlet or even in Yeats's next volume, *The Wild Swans at Coole*, which came out in 1919. Lady Gregory realized how dangerous the poem was; she did not want it published. She had uncorked the genie by writing to Yeats in August about his future role and influence; now she sought to put it back in the bottle. On 28 March 1917, six months after he wrote the poem, when Yeats arranged to have twenty-five copies printed to be distributed to close friends, he wrote to the printer: "Please be very careful with the Rebellion poem. Lady Gregory asked me not to send it to you until we had finalized our dispute with the authorities about the Lane pictures. She was afraid of it getting about and damaging us and she is not timid."

Lady Gregory's nephew Hugh Lane, to whom she had become very close, died when the *Lusitania* was torpedoed off the coast of Cork in May 1915. Bernard Shaw was staying at Coole, and her son Robert was home on leave. Shaw asked her what he could do to help her. "I said I longed to be alone, to cry, to moan, to scream if I wished. I wanted to be out of hearing and out of sight. Robert came and was terribly distressed, he had been so used to my composure."

Lane's will, which was found in London, left his valuable collection of pictures to the National Gallery of England. But, on Lady Gregory's suggestion, his desk at the National Gallery in Dublin, where he had become director in 1914, was searched and an unsigned codicil to his will was found which left the paintings to Dublin and named Lady Gregory as his trustee. She worked until her death in 1932 to get the paintings back to Ireland. Over and over she travelled to London to see the great and the good; she tirelessly wrote letters and lobbied. (She even wrote to George Moore.) She enlisted the help of Sir Edward Carson and Augustine Birrell, who had been Chief Secretary in Dublin during the 1916 Rising. All her old contacts in London came in useful. She had moved in the 1890s from unionism to support for Home Rule. Now, after the Rising, she was in the rebel camp, even though her son Robert was in the British Army and part of a world that viewed the Rising as an abject piece of treachery, even though she was in London talking as though nothing had changed.

The publication of "Easter 1916" would threaten the ambiguity under which she had sheltered. The plays she and Yeats had written had not been a direct celebration of recent rebellion; they were rooted in history and could be read as metaphor. And even though "Easter 1916" had several passages that expressed ambivalence about the Rising, the poem's listing of the leaders and its refrain were what people would notice and remember. On Lady Gregory's insistence, the poem's publication was deferred; although Yeats read it aloud a few times to friends, it did not appear in print until 17 March 1919, when *The Irish Commonwealth*, a Dublin magazine, quoted the first sixteen lines, and it was not published in England until October 1920, when it appeared in its entirety in *The New Statesman*.

Four of her Persse nephews were killed in the fighting in France. In almost all of her letters to Yeats during the war, there was some reference to her son Robert, who had become a pilot. In June 1917 she wrote: "Robert, having been given Legion of Honour for France, has now been given military cross for England. He must have been very brave and very efficient out there. He is at Salisbury now, trying out the new machines and there is to be flight instruction for a bit." Later, she wrote about the new planes: "The machines are single-engine, he will be alone with a machine gun." In October 1917 she wrote: "And there is only half of me here while Robert is in danger. He is in France this week inspecting aerodromes, flying from one to another." Soon, he moved to Italy. In December 1917 she wrote: "We had a cheery letter from Robert from Milan ... There is danger everywhere."

A month later, Robert was shot down in error by an Italian pilot as he returned from a mission, although Lady Gregory never knew about the error. She was alone in Coole when the news came and had to make her way by train to Galway to tell Margaret, Robert's wife. "I stood there and Margaret came in. She cried at once 'Is he dead?' ... Then I sat down on the floor and cried."

Yeats wrote four poems on the death of Robert Gregory; two of them are among his greatest. The circumstances of the composition of all four poems, and Lady Gregory's close monitoring of them, remain the most astonishing and telling episode in their long relationship. She wrote to him on 2 February 1918: "If you feel like it some time – write something down that we may keep – you understood him better than many." A few days later she wrote to Yeats about Margaret's wishes for him to do something: "If you would send even a paragraph — just something of what I know you are feeling — to the Observer — or failing that the Nation — she would feel it a comfort." She enclosed notes for him about Robert. Yeats wrote to John Quinn: "I think he had genius. Certainly no contemporary landscape moved me as much as two or three of his, except perhaps a certain landscape by Innes, from whom he had learned a good deal. His paintings had majesty and austerity, and at the same time sweetness. He was the most accomplished man I have ever known; he could do more things than any other." Yeats also wrote to Iseult Gonne that Robert Gregory had "a strange pure genius ... I have always felt that he had a luckless star and have expected the end." He wrote a piece for the *Observer* saying that Robert Gregory's "very accomplishment hid from many his genius. He had so many sides that some among his friends were not sure what his work would be."

Yeats wrote to John Quinn, saying that his real grief was for Lady Gregory. In his first poem about Robert Gregory, "Shepherd and Goatherd", Yeats's invocation of Lady Gregory at Coole is among his most pedestrian work:

> *She goes about her house erect and calm*
> *Between the pantry and the linen chest,*
> *Or else at meadow or at grazing overlooks*

> *Her labouring men, as though her darling lived,*
> *But for her grandson now* [...]

The poem goes on to deal with Robert, how he had built no house in his lifetime and left merely a few paintings. It cannot have offered Lady Gregory much consolation when Yeats showed it to her on his arrival in Coole in April 1918. The dead artist, he wrote:

> [...] *left the house as in his father's time*
> *As though he knew himself, as it were, a cuckoo,*
> *No settled man. And now that he is gone*
> *There's nothing of him left but half a score*
> *Of sorrowful, austere, sweet, lofty pipe tunes.*

In a letter to his wife, which John Kelly quotes in *Lady Gregory: Fifty Years After*, Yeats, who had begun to write "In Memory of Major Robert Gregory" at Coole, wrote: "I have done nothing but ... discuss with Lady Gregory the new stanza that is to commend Robert's courage in the hunting field. It has been a little thorny but we have settled a compromise. I have got from her a list of musical place-names where he hunted ... I have firmly resisted all suggested eloquence about aero planes '& the blue Italian sky'. It is pathetic for Lady Gregory constantly says that it [the poem] is his monument – 'all that remains'."

The pathos of the poem "In Memory of Major Robert Gregory" comes not from the qualities claimed for Robert Gregory, which are exaggerated, but from the withholding of his name until the sixth line of the sixth stanza. In many journal entries between now and her death, Lady Gregory also withheld her dead son's name, referring to "the grave in Italy" or "the grave in Padua" or "my darling". Now, in Yeats's poem, other names can be mentioned – the poet Lionel Johnson, the playwright Synge, Yeats's uncle George Pollexfen – but since the poem is called "In Memory of Major Robert Gregory", we know that these names are being mentioned only because the poem cannot bring itself to mention the real name, the name that is unsayable in the body of the poem. The poet is accustomed to the "lack of breath" of those he has named,

> *But not that my dear friend's dear son*
> *Our Sidney and our perfect man*
> *Could share in that discourtesy of death.*

In the last stanza, the poet says that he thought to comment on more of his friends, "but the thought / Of that late death took all my heart for speech". The poem will delay as long as possible coming to its point, just as Lady Gregory in January 1918 on her way to Galway to tell

Margaret that Robert was dead desperately wanted to postpone the moment when it would have to be said. ("In the train," she wrote, "I felt it was cruel to be going so quickly to break Margaret's heart, I wished the train would go slower ... It was agony knowing the journey was at an end.") Yeats, too, wants the poem to go slower, to hold the telling. But once it's said, then it is too sad to go on, no other dead friends can be summoned up. Thus he did not merely obey Lady Gregory's request to put the names of places like Esserkelly or Moneen into the poem; he sought to follow in his poem the shape of her grief.

In much of Yeats's poetry, there are two voices: one is public, it is there to persuade; the other is private and whispering, a poetry of the night. Often the same poem comes in these two guises – "September 1913" and "The Fisherman", for example, or "Sailing to Byzantium" and "Byzantium" – and now too, along with the public poem "In Memory of Major Robert Gregory", a poem to be read aloud to a group, came its whispered counterpart, a sixteen-line poem told in the first person by Robert Gregory, "An Irish Airman Foresees His Death". And this, too, after the tactlessness of "Shepherd and Goatherd", sought to console Lady Gregory, after all she had done for her country, that Robert had died in a war not Ireland's. The poem rid Robert of imperial will, or English patriotism. It changed the "Major" into "An Irish Airman". It made him abstractly heroic: his "lonely impulse of delight / Drove to this tumult in the clouds". It handed him back to Coole which the war could not touch, the house his mother had guarded for him:

> *My country is Kiltartan Cross,*
> *My countrymen Kiltartan's poor,*
> *No likely end could bring them loss*
> *Or leave them happier than before.*

The fourth poem, eventually entitled "Reprisals", is the strangest. As the terrible beauty of the 1916 Rising made its way into guerilla war in 1919 and 1920, Lady Gregory was in Coole and Yeats either in Dublin or in England. Her journals for the period remain one of the best accounts of the daily and nightly terror unleashed by the Black and Tans, whom the British had sent to pacify Ireland. She wrote a number of articles for *The Nation* in London, making clear what was happening in Ireland. She did not sign the articles, but it was known among the republican leadership that she had written them. This, and her generally good relationship with the locals, meant that Coole was not endangered. She viewed the violence of the rampaging British with horror. She also viewed the poem Yeats sent her from Oxford in November 1920 with horror. He initially entitled it "To Major Robert Gregory, airman":

> *Considering that before you died*
> *You had brought down some nineteen planes,*
> *I think that you were satisfied,*
> *And life at last seemed worth the pains.*
> *'I have had more happiness in one year*
> *Than in all the other years,' you said;*
> *And battle joy may be so dear*
> *A memory even to the dead*
> *It chases common thought away.*

> *Yet rise from your Italian tomb,*
> *Flit to Kiltartan Cross and stay*
> *Till certain second thought have come*
> *Upon the cause you served, that we*
> *Imagined such a fine affair:*
> *Half-drunk or whole-mad soldiery*
> *Are murdering your tenants there;*
> *Men that revere your father yet*
> *Are shot at on the open plain;*
> *Where can new-married women sit*
> *To suckle children now? Armed men*
> *May murder them in passing by*
> *Nor parliament, nor law take heed: —*
> *Then stop your ears with dust and lie*
> *Among the other cheated dead.*
>
> *November 23 1920*

"My dear Lady Gregory," he wrote in his customary greeting (she always wrote "Dear Willie"), "I send you this a new poem to Robert. I am sending it at once to The Times and if they will not have it, I will send it to The Nation." He mentioned that he had not asked her leave, but added that the poem was "good, good for its purpose". On the envelope, which is in the Berg Collection in the New York Public Library, she wrote: "I did not like this and asked not to have it published." In her journal she wrote: "Yeats writes enclosing lines he has written and has, without telling me, sent to The Times, I dislike them – I cannot bear the dragging of R. from his grave to make what I think a not very sincere poem – for Yeats only knows by hearsay while our troubles go on – and he quoted words G.B.S. told him and did not mean him to repeat – and which will give pain – I hardly know why it gives me extraordinary pain and it seems too late to stop it ... and I fear the night."

Shaw had written to her about Robert: "When I met Robert at the flying station on the west point, in abominably cold weather, with a frostbite on his face hardly healed, he told me that the six months he had been there had been the happiest of his life. An amazing thing to say considering his exceptionally fortunate circumstances at home; but he evidently meant it." This idea that the adventure of the war had made Robert happier than his childhood at Coole or his marriage would not have been a great consolation to his mother or his widow or his three children. Nor that he was among the "cheated dead". Nor, indeed, that he "had brought down some nineteen planes". Lady Gregory managed to stop the poem being published. It did not appear in any periodical of the time, nor in any collection by Yeats. It was first printed in a magazine in 1948 when they were both dead.

Lady Gregory continued to read manuscripts submitted to the Abbey, alert always to possible new talent, but also, especially as the new state was coming into being, to the political implications of a new play. Thus in November 1921 she noted in her journal a play called "The Crimson and the Tricolour" by Sean O'Casey. "This is a puzzling play," she wrote, "extremely interesting … It is the expression of ideas that makes it interesting (besides feeling that the writer has something in him) & no doubt the point of interest for Dublin audiences. But we could not put it on while the Revolution is still unaccomplished – it might hasten the Labour attack on Sinn Fein, which ought to be kept back til the fight with England is over, & the new Government has had time to show what it can do." She decided to have the play typed at the theatre's expense. She met the writer five days later and remarked in her journal that he was "a strong Labour man" who nonetheless said that if his play would weaken Sinn Féin then he "would be the last to wish to put it on". Yeats, in any case, did not like the play and it was turned down. He thought that it was "so constructed that in every scene there is something for pit and stalls to cheer and boo. In fact it is the old Irish idea of a good play … especially as everybody is as ill-mannered as possible & all truth considered as inseparable from spite and hatred." Robinson sent this critique to O'Casey, who dismissed Yeats's objection to his play.

In November 1922 the Abbey accepted O'Casey's play *The Shadow of a Gunman*. Lady Gregory and he shared an earnestness and a belief in duty, a belief that mankind could be improved and Ireland could be helped too. Sometimes, in her journal, when she quoted him, his aims and ambitions sounded very close to her own: "Now his desire and hope is rather to lead the workers into a better life ... in drama especially." As good Protestants, they had both read their bibles in youth and they discussed the beauty of the language. On the opening night, 12 April 1923, O'Casey saw the play from the side wings only, but the next night Lady Gregory sat with him in the theatre, having brought him – she called him "Casey" in her journals – "round to the door before the play to share my joy at seeing the crowd surging in". He said to her that "all the thought in Ireland for years past has come through the Abbey. You have no idea what an education it has been for the country."

That, she said, put her "in great spirits", but more important perhaps was the fact that they liked each other. Later, he wrote: "I loved her, and I think she was very fond of me – why, God only knows. Our friendship-affinity was an odd one: she from affluence, I from poverty; she an aristocrat, I a proletarian Communist. Yet, we understood each other well, talking, eating, and laughing easily together."

In March 1924 *Juno and the Paycock* opened at the Abbey. "A long queue at the door," Lady Gregory wrote in her journal, "the theatre crowded, many turned away, so it will be run on next week. A wonderful and terrible play of futility, of irony, humour, tragedy." O'Casey now told her that he was glad she had turned down his earlier play. "I owe a great deal to you and Mr Yeats and Mr Robinson," she reported him saying, "but to you above all. You gave me encouragement. And it was you who said to me upstairs in the office – I could show you the very spot where you stood – 'Mr O'Casey, your gift is characterisation'. And so I threw over my theories and worked at characters, and this is the result." Yeats said the play reminded him of Tolstoy. Lady Gregory recorded in her journal that she said to him: "This is one of the evenings at the Abbey that makes one glad to be born."

Lady Gregory took Sean O'Casey to one of Yeats's Monday nights. "He is studying pictures now," she wrote, "has bought some books but knows so little about painting he wishes lectures could be given, 'And if the employers cared for us workers they could sometimes arrange for an afternoon at the Galleries, or an evening at the Abbey for their men.'" On 7 June that year O'Casey made his first visit to Coole. "I am alone," Lady Gregory had written, "& have no amusements to offer, but I think you would find the library an interest, it is a good one." She met him at Athenry and they travelled together third class – she always travelled third class – to Gort. He loved the house and the woods, but almost fell asleep when she read to him at night. Both of them have left accounts of the visit. O'Casey, in Lady Gregory's journal-version, spoke to her about his mother and his grief at her death, told her of his learning to read, his communism. She read to him from Thomas Hardy's *The Dynasts*. "He is tremendously struck with it," she wrote. "He is very happy walking in the woods and dipping into the books in the library."

O'Casey devoted a chapter to Lady Gregory in the fourth volume of his autobiography, *Inishfallen Fare Thee Well*, published in 1949. He called the chapter "Blessed Bridget O'Coole". She was, he wrote, "a sturdy, stout little figure soberly clad in solemn black, made gay with a touch of something white ... Her face was a rugged one, hardy as that of a peasant, curiously lit with an odd dignity, and softened with a careless touch of humour in the bright eyes and the curving wrinkles crowding around the corners of the firm little mouth. She looked like an old, elegant nun of a new order, a blend of the Lord Jesus Christ and of Puck, an order that Ireland had never known before and wasn't likely to know again for a long time to come."

Another account of O'Casey's visit to Coole was written by Anne Gregory in her book *Me and Nu: Childhood at Coole*. She recounted the shock among the staff at O'Casey's attire: " 'Great playwright is it?' Marian snorted, drawing herself up, her starched apron creaking, her white cap quivering with fury. 'Great playwright? I'll give him great playwright. What right at all has a man like that to come into Coole without a tie on his collar, nor a collar on his shirt.'"

In the end Lady Gregory prevailed on the playwright to wear a "neckchief". Anne Gregory and her sister continued to observe the visitor carefully: "We were both fascinated by him, for though Grandma had told us about him having taught himself to read and write, and that he had written such a brilliant play, we hadn't realised that he would have such a terrific Dublin accent. We couldn't believe that anyone who talked like that could write at all, let alone write brilliant plays, and we listened intently as he and Grandma talked and talked over lunch and tea."

In November 1923 Yeats won the Nobel Prize. In a draft of his acceptance speech, which he showed to Lady Gregory, he had written that the prize should have been shared with Synge and with "an old woman sinking into the infirmities of age". ("Not even fighting them," she wrote in her journal.) She asked Yeats to amend his remark, which could, she thought, "be considered to mean that I had gone silly". In his final version, he wrote of "a living woman sinking into the infirmity of age".

There was always that mixture in their relationship of

complete empathy and bouts of tactlessness on his side, and a mixture of possessiveness and a willingness to stand up to him on her side. "It is strange," she wrote to him in January 1914, "I had a very bad dream last night, I dreamt you were dying, lying in a bed, crumbling to earth as I looked at you. I awoke quite distressed and troubled." In that same month, she read his new collection of poems *Responsibilities* and wrote to him: "I read through the poems last night, I think they will make a fine volume and send your reputation up higher than ever. 'The Grey Rock' is the one I care most for, but I like all except 'Friends'. I don't like being catalogued." In "Friends", the poet named three woman who "have wrought / What joy is in my days". The first was Olivia Shakespear, with whom he had had an affair; the last was Maud Gonne. Lady Gregory was in the middle:

> *And one because her hand*
> *Had strength that could unbind*
> *What none can understand,*
> *What none can have and thrive,*
> *Youth's dreamy load, till she*
> *So changed me that I live*
> *Labouring in ecstasy.*

Despite his praise for the strength of her hand, he did not much rate her as an artist. In November 1924 she recorded him telling her that her play *The Image* was "rubbish". In his *Memoirs,* he wrote: "Being a writer for comedy, her life as an artist has not shaken in her, as tragic art would have done, the conventional standards. Besides, she has never been part of the artist's world, she has belonged to a political world, or one that is merely social." In his categories of people in his book *A Vision,* he placed her with John Galsworthy and Queen Victoria. ("But I don't think she could have written 'Seven Short Plays'," Lady Gregory commented.) In 1931, when Lady Gregory was in Dublin for medical treatment and was staying with the Yeatses, George Yeats, who had married W.B. Yeats in 1917, wrote to Dorothy Shakespear, who was married to Ezra Pound: "Since then – that's eleven days ago – life has been a perpetual fro and to and to and fro ... Christ, how she repeats herself ... she'll tell you the same saga quite literally three times in less than an hour, and repeats it the next day, and the day after that too."

As the new Irish state came into being, both Lady Gregory and Yeats needed all their social and political skills to ensure the survival of the Abbey and indeed their own survival. Yeats became a senator in the Free State and during the Civil War needed an armed guard on his house. Lady Gregory refused an offer of a seat in the Senate at first and then in 1925 let her name go forward for election, but did no canvassing and was not elected. She was alone at Coole for some of the time watching the children of her peaceful tenants becoming radical and unruly. She wrote to Yeats: "I think the division in politics draws a pretty clear line between fathers and sons about here." In 1920, when she saw six or eight young men in her woods and they did not stop when she told them to, she wrote in her journal: "I felt terribly upset – it seemed like what we had heard of the French Revolution as it began and lately in Russia, the peasants making themselves free of the woods." Two years later, when a tenant made demands on her, she showed him "how easy it would be to shoot me through the unshuttered window if he wanted to use violence". Yeats referred to this in "Beautiful Lofty Things":

Augusta Gregory seated at her great ormolu table,
Her eightieth winter approaching: 'Yesterday he threatened my life.
I told him that nightly from six to seven I sat at this table,
The blinds drawn up' [...]

During the Civil War Lady Gregory had a mastectomy and spent time recovering at the Yeatses' house in Merrion Square. With Yeats, she saw a great deal of the first government, even though her secret sympathies lay with the republican side. As the new state was formed, Yeats and

Lady Gregory decided the best way to ensure the theatre's future was to offer it to the state; there were many discussions and negotiations. In the end, it was decided that the state would subsidize the theatre, rather than take it over, but the price of the subsidy was a government representative, the economist George O'Brien, on the board of the theatre. This was the context in which Yeats and Lady Gregory's last great battle about censorship and freedom of expression would take place.

In August 1925 O'Casey submitted his new play *The Plough and the Stars*, which dealt with Easter Week 1916, to the Abbey. Yeats and Lennox Robinson and Lady Gregory liked the play ("she is an extraordinarily broad-minded woman", O'Casey wrote to a friend) and it was to be staged in February 1926. By early September there were problems. One of the players wrote to Lady Gregory: "At any time I would think twice before having anything to do with it. The language is – to use an Abbey phrase – beyond the beyonds. The song at the end of the second Act sung by the 'girl-of-the-streets' is impossible." In rehearsal some of the actors objected to individual lines, one having been forbidden by her confessor to say them. The play allowed Irish nationalists to mix with prostitutes; it also showed a Tricolour being brought into a pub. But the overall message of the play was even more offensive: it did not glorify those who fought for Irish freedom at a time when many of them were hungry for glory. Soon, the play was read by George O'Brien, the government representative on the board, who wrote of "the possibility that the play might offend any section of public opinion so seriously as to provoke an attack on the Theatre of a kind that would endanger the continuance of the subsidy". In his letter to Yeats he listed words which he though should be removed (these included "Jesus", "Jasus" and "Christ" as well as "bitch", "lowsers" and "lice"). Of the presence of the prostitute, he wrote that "the lady's professional side is unduly emphasized". The tone of his letter suggested that he was within his rights to demand the removal of words, characters and undue emphasis.

When Yeats came to Coole to discuss this, Lady Gregory, according to her journal, "said at once that our position is clear. If we have to choose between the subsidy and our freedom, it is our freedom we choose. And we must tell him that there was no condition attached to the subsidy." She and Yeats did, however, discuss cutting the offensive song from the play. At the subsequent directors' meeting, Lady Gregory gave George O'Brien a lecture on the theatre's battles with censorship. O'Brien still wanted the song removed. "We had already decided it must go, but left it as a bone for him to gnaw at," Lady Gregory wrote.

On 11 February there was a riot in the theatre. Lady Gregory was at Coole and read about it in the newspaper on her way to Dublin. Yeats had been in the theatre and had addressed the audience, who had difficulty hearing him, from the stage. However, he sent his speech to the *Irish Times*: "You have disgraced yourselves again ... Is this ... going to be a recurring celebration of Irish genius? Synge first and then O'Casey! The news of the happening of the last few minutes here will flash from country to country. Dublin has once more rocked the cradle of a reputation. From such a scene in this theatre, went forth the fame of Synge. Equally, the fame of O'Casey is born here tonight. This is his apotheosis."

Yeats met Lady Gregory at the station. He wanted to have another debate, as they did after the *Playboy* riots, but she realized that this was different: many of the rioters were women who had lost men in 1916 and the War of Independence; they were not the rabble, and they would always have the support of the public. Some of them owned toothbrushes. They were led by the ardent republican Hanna Sheehy Skeffington, whose husband had been shot in the Rising while trying to prevent looting, and they included Maud Gonne MacBride. Lady Gregory had very little time for women, and no interest in debating with them. In 1906 she wrote to John Quinn: "I should be content to have Jack Yeats and Douglas Hyde here for six months of the year, but a few weeks of their wives makes me hide in the woods! And I have felt the same with AE and his wife." She had a rule, which she wrote down in her journal for 29 September 1919, "of never talking of politics with a woman". Five years later her position had not changed, as she believed that the badness of the newspaper *Sinn Féin* was a result of there being "too many women on it". Thus there was no Abbey debate. Four years after her death, Yeats wrote that "Lady Gregory never rebelled like other Irish women I have known, who consumed themselves and their friends". Wilfrid Scawen Blunt wrote of her: "She is the only woman I have known of real intellectual power equal to men and that without having anything unnaturally masculine about her."

Mrs Sheehy Skeffington, however, was eager for more rebellion and wrote to the newspapers: "In no country save in Ireland could a State-subsidised theatre presume on popular patience to the extent of making a mockery and a byword of a revolutionary movement on which the present structure claims to stand." She and O'Casey had a spirited debate in the newspapers, but O'Casey became ill during a public debate with her, partly, he said, because of the sight of Maud Gonne MacBride, "the colonel's daughter still". Also, a number of younger writers who disliked Yeats now took this opportunity to dislike O'Casey; among them were Liam O'Flaherty and Austin Clarke.

Once more, despite the opposition from the republican widows and the government representative on the board and the young writers who disliked him, Yeats and Lady Gregory prevailed. The theatre was packed; the play was not taken off, nor the subsidy removed. In the early years of the Irish state, the production of *The Plough and the Stars* stood almost alone as a blow for freedom of expression.

The rejection of *The Silver Tassie* in April 1928 and the consequent alienation of O'Casey stands alone in Lady Gregory's career as an example of mismanagement and short-sightedness. The play was read by Robinson in Dublin and Lady Gregory in Coole, and was sent to Yeats in Italy, but he did not read it until his return to Dublin. The fourth director, Walter Starkie, who had replaced George O'Brien on the board, was in Spain. None of them liked it but they did not meet to discuss what they should do with it. Instead, Yeats wrote in his magisterial style: "There is no dominating character, no dominating action, neither psychological unity nor unity of action." He wrote to Lady Gregory suggesting that O'Casey, to save face, should withdraw the play. O'Casey, in the meantime, was in England, where his first child had just been born; he was so sure that the theatre intended to produce his play that he had suggested a cast-list to Robinson and was preparing the text for publication. Instead, Lady Gregory sent him Yeats's report, making clear that his view was "what we all think", although Walter Starkie had still not given his view. (He thought they should produce the play.) She noted in her journal for Saturday 23 April: "Of course it must be a severe blow, but I believe he will feel its force, its 'integrity' and be grateful in the end ... But I had a bad night, or early morning, thinking of the disappointment and shock he will feel."

O'Casey was not grateful. He wrote to Robinson in a rage at Yeats's suggestion that he should withdraw the play to save face: "There is going to be no damned secrecy with me surrounding the Abbey's rejection of the play. Does he think that I would practise in my life the prevarication and wretchedness that I laugh at in my plays?" Some of the correspondence was published in the *Observer* in June 1928 and the rest in the *Irish Statesman* a week later.

Lady Gregory never saw O'Casey again, although they maintained a formal and sporadic correspondence until her death in 1932. She came to regret what had happened. "It is the only occasion I can recollect", Lennox Robinson wrote, "when on some important matter of opinion or policy she did change her mind." On her last visit to London in April 1931 she expressed a wish to meet O'Casey again and see his wife and son, but he did not want to meet her. Finally, on 30 October 1931, she wrote to him from Coole: "I don't think I am likely to cross the Channel again, for I am at present crippled by a rheumatic attack, and at my age it is not likely to pass away ... Perhaps one day you will bring your wife here. I am sorry not to have met her."

In his autobiography, despite everything that had happened, Sean O'Casey recited Lady Gregory's praises: "Not Yeats, nor Martyn, nor Miss Horniman gave the Abbey Theatre its enduring life, but this woman only, with the rugged cheeks, high upper lip, twinkling eyes, pricked with a dot of steel in their centres; this woman only, who in the midst of venomous opposition, served as a general runabout in sensible pride and lofty humility."

As the 1920s went on, however, neither her pride nor her humility allowed her to keep up with the times. Neither she nor Yeats paid any attention to developments in the European theatre. They had supervised one theatrical revolution; they were not ready to pay attention to another. This may go some way towards explaining their failure to appreciate the expressionist central act in *The Silver Tassie*. In 1927 a clever young playwright named Denis Johnston submitted his "Shadowdance" to the Abbey, thus giving the perplexed directors something new and strange to mull over. The dialogue in the opening of the play was entirely made up of lines from nationalist ballads and speeches, cliché rendered into hilarious claptrap, thus making Cathleen Ní Houlihan and all who sailed in her seem ridiculous. The rest of the play was a vicious and energetic parody of Irish nationalism. Almost nine months passed without a word from Lennox Robinson or Yeats or Lady Gregory.

Johnston did not suffer pieties gladly. He was sophisticated and clever, from the Dublin Protestant upper-middle class. He had not enjoyed the Irish Civil War and its many causes. He was ready to be an *enfant terrible* in the new Irish state, taking a dim view of its central beliefs and its theatrical hierarchy. "I was never invited to Gort," he wrote as though it were a badge of honour.

In 1928 the Abbey invited him to direct *King Lear*, but he still heard nothing about "Shadowdance". One day, however, as they were walking from Lennox Robinson's house to the bus stop in Dalkey, Yeats finally spoke. "We both seemed rather embarrassed", Johnston wrote, "as we walked a long way in silence. Finally he said 'I liked your play, but it has one or two faults. Firstly, the scenes I thought were too long.' He turned for a while and gazed at a coal boat in the Dalkey sound. 'Then,' he continued, 'there are too many scenes. If we put on this play we would annoy our audience and lose £50. We do not much mind the £50, but we do not want to annoy our audience. So we're prepared to give you the £50 to put it on for yourself."

His manuscript was returned, much stained and annotated. A stray poem by Yeats was left among the pages. And, according to Johnston in the 1960 edition of his *Collected Plays*, someone had written "The Old Lady Says No" on the title-page, though this has been disputed and Johnston may have invented the title. Johnston had met Lady

Gregory, the old lady in question, in "the back sitting room of her hotel in Harcourt Street", according to himself, and she had expressed "distaste" for the play and described the opening playlet as "coarse". It seems from Johnston's account that she did not realize that the play was an elaborate joke. But it was clear, in any case, that she did not like it. Johnston took his play to the newly founded Gate Theatre, and the Abbey Theatre began its decline.

Lady Gregory did not own Coole. Once Robert came of age in 1902, it was his, and when he was killed it was inherited by his widow Margaret. In her journals between 1918 and her death, Lady Gregory wrote almost every day about her three grandchildren, who stayed with her during holidays. She believed that Coole should now be preserved for Richard, who would be twenty-one in 1930, just as she had once preserved the estate for Robert. She continued to love Coole. In February 1924 she wrote in her journal: "last night in the library the firelight, the lamplight, shining on the rich bindings of that wall of books; and this evening, by the lake, so silent and beautiful, Cranagh so peaceful — 'the tilled familiar land'; and later as I went upstairs and looked from my window at the sunset behind the blue range of hills, I felt so grateful, as I have often done of late, to my husband who brought me to this house and home".

Her disputes with her daughter-in-law also pepper her diaries. Margaret wanted to sell not only the land, but the house and the furniture as well, and was shocked to discover that Lady Gregory owned much of the furniture. There was no open warfare between them, merely disagreements and assertions of rights. They also admired each other, and after Lady Gregory's death, in her dealings with both Yeats and Lennox Robinson, Margaret made clear her resentment of how her mother-in-law had been undervalued. In 1928, with Lady Gregory's blessing ("I believe Robert would be, or is, glad"), Margaret married Guy Gough of the neighbouring estate Cutra (who had lit the bonfire for Queen Victoria in 1897).

After the sale to the Ministry of Lands and Agriculture on 1 April 1927, Lady Gregory rented back the house and gardens for a hundred pounds a year. She wrote to Yeats in October: "The Commissioners are coming to take over the place. I feel rather downhearted. I know it can't be helped as Margaret has long set her heart on selling and I don't think I should be able to go on taking the burden of expense and management very much longer – yet it is a break, almost a defeat – there are so few houses left."

She enjoyed offering hospitality to any member of the Free State government who came to a play at the Abbey;

she continued to supervise affairs at the theatre throughout her seventies. In October 1921 she was having a meeting in the Mansion House in Dublin when she mentioned to the Lord Mayor that she had never seen Eamon de Valera "and would much like to see him, even from the window". When de Valera appeared she was hurried to the doorway and introduced to him. "I said I was just going to his old constituency, west Clare, and he said that he had never had time to go there since just after his first election, and I said there were many very proud of having had him as a representative." She told him that he had been "so often in my prayers I wanted to see what you looked like". She liked his face, "good, honest, with something of Lincoln".

In the year of her death, he took power in Ireland and held it for almost a quarter of a century. The ideology on which he based his politics was essentially hers, but without her liberalism and her belief in the aristocracy, and, because it was politics, ready to accept failure. It stressed rural values and an ideal Ireland; it exalted those who had lived frugally and traditionally. It spurned material and economic interests. Her dream Ireland began in stories and books and plays, but it ended in politics. She managed to inhabit two ideologies – that of landlord and that of nationalist – at the same time; so, too, de Valera managed his policies on partition and the Irish language and self-sufficiency with a masterly ambiguity.

In 1959 de Valera became President of Ireland, and for fourteen years he would inhabit the old Viceregal Lodge, now Áras an Uachtaráin. Lady Gregory knew the building; it was here she had faced down Lord Aberdeen over *Blanco Posnet*. Since the early days of the Abbey Theatre she had refused to accept invitations here, even when the representatives of the Crown offered not to publish her name as a guest. When Tim Healy became Governor-General of the Free State, Yeats had written a formal letter to His Excellency asking for a meeting. Healy had replied: "My dear Boy, come and see me whenever you like in the 'bee-loud glade'."

In 1928 Healy was replaced by James MacNeill, who invited Lady Gregory to stay in the house on a number of occasions. She wrote in her journal: "The thought came to me that a hundred years ago, 1828, William, my husband, may very likely have been playing about in these rooms and terraces, a boy of twelve." In February 1929 she came with her granddaughter Catherine. As they were shown around the house, Lady Gregory said that Catherine's grandfather, Sir William, had come to this house when his own grandfather was Under-Secretary and also lived in the Phoenix Park. Sir William had learned his Latin lessons from the Viceroy, Lord Wellesley, in these rooms. In these rooms too, Sir William as a boy had asked the future Lord Melbourne for a stick of sealing wax and had been told: "That's right. Begin life early. All these things belong to the public, and your business must always be to get out of the public as much as you can."

Lady Gregory had done the opposite. And now she was in a unique position in the new state. She, whose family was steeped in the history of Anglo-Irish power, was welcome in the house of the Irish governor-general that had been the seat of English power for so long. Others who came from her class and espoused the cause of Irish nationalism were too extreme now and opposed the compromises that the new state had made. Most of her class had left the country. She was skilled in the politics of compromise and was a superb tactician. But her eye remained on her goal: to establish Ireland's ancient past as part of its present culture and to produce contemporary Irish masterpieces in an Irish theatre. She put all her steely energy into this and she succeeded, turning a blind eye to the parts of her own heritage that did not suit her purpose. She lived in two worlds: one of them became the Irish Free State and she was proud of that. The other one disappeared. In 1930, Richard had his twenty-first birthday at Coole. "But it is a contrast", she wrote, "to Robert's coming of age, with the gathering of cousins and the big feast and dance for the tenants – Coole no longer ours. But the days of landed gentry have passed. It is better so. Yet I wish some one of our blood would after my death care enough for what has been a home for so long, to keep it open."

Sources

ARCHIVAL SOURCES

Lady Gregory papers, Berg Collection, New York Public Library
John Quinn Memorial Collection, New York Public Library

PRINTED SOURCES

Adams, Bernard. *Denis Johnston: A Life*, Dublin, 2002.

Blunt, Wilfrid Scawen. *Poetical Works*, London, 1914.

Coxhead, Elizabeth. *Lady Gregory: A Literary Portrait*, London, 1961.

Donoghue, Denis, ed. *W.B. Yeats: Memoirs*, London, 1972.

Ellmann, Richard. *James Joyce*, Oxford, 1982.

Ellmann, Richard, ed. *Selected Letters of James Joyce*, New York, 1975.

Foster, R.F. *W.B. Yeats: A Life*, Volume 1, Oxford, 1997.

Foster, R.F. *Paddy and Mr Punch*, London, 1993.

Glendinning, Victoria. *Trollope*, London, 1992.

Greene, David H., and Edward M. Stephens. *J.M. Synge*, New York, 1959.

Gregory, Anne. *Me and Nu: Childhood in Coole*, Gerrards Cross, 1970.

Gregory, Lady. *Cuchulain of Muirthemne*, London, 1902.

Gregory, Lady. *Diaries 1892–1902*, ed. James Pethica, Oxford, 1996.

Gregory, Lady. *Journals*, vol. II, ed. Daniel J. Murphy, New York, 1987.

Gregory, Lady. *Lady Gregory's Journals 1916–1930*, ed. Lennox Robinson, New York, 1947.

Gregory, Lady. *Our Irish Theatre*, London, 1913.

Gregory, Lady. *Selected Plays*, Gerrards Cross, 1975.

Sources

Gregory, Lady. *Seventy Years*. Gerrards Cross, 1976.

Gregory, Lady, ed. *Sir William Gregory: An Autobiography*, London, 1894.

Gregory, Lady. *Visions and Beliefs in the West of Ireland*, New York, 1970.

Guest, Lady Charlotte, trs. *The Mabinogion*, London, 1980.

Gwynn, Stephen. *Irish Literature and Drama*, London, 1936.

Hobsbawm, Eric, and Terence Ranger, eds. *The Invention of Tradition*, Cambridge, 1983.

Holroyd, Michael. *Bernard Shaw*, Volume II, London, 1989.

Hyde, Douglas. *Beside the Fire*, New York, 1973.

Jenkins, Brian. *Sir William Gregory of Coole: The Biography of an Anglo-Irishman*, Gerrards Cross, 1986.

Johnston, Denis. *Collected Plays*, vol. I, London, 1960.

Joyce, James. *A Portrait of the Artist as a Young Man*, London, 1992.

Kohfeldt, Mary Lou. *Lady Gregory: The Woman Behind the Irish Renaissance*, New York, 1985.

Krause, David. *Sean O'Casey: The Man and His Work*, New York, 1975.

Krause, David, ed. *The Letters of Sean O'Casey*, Volume I, New York, 1975.

Krause, David, and Robert G. Lowery, eds. *Sean O'Casey: Centenary Essays*, Gerrards Cross, 1988.

Longford, Elizabeth. *A Pilgrimage of Passion: The Life of Wilfri,nd Scawen Blunt*, London, 1979.

Mason, Ellsworth, and Richard Ellmann, eds. *The Critical Writings of James Joyce*, New York, 1959.

Mikhail, E.H, ed. *Lady Gregory: Interviews and Recollections*, London, 1977.

Moore, George. *Hail and Farewell*, New York, 1925.

Murphy, William M. *Prodigal Father: The Life of John Butler Yeats*, Ithaca, 1978.

O'Casey, Sean. *Inishfallen Fare Thee Well*, London, 1949.

O'Connor, Garry. *Sean O'Casey: A Life*, London, 1988

O'Grady, Standish Hayes. *Silva Gadelica*, New York, 1970.

O'Grady, Standish James. *History of Ireland*, New York, 1970.

O'Rourke, Canon John, *The Great Irish Famine*, Dublin, 1989.

Reid, B.L. *The Man from New York: John Quinn and his Friends*, New York, 1968.

Saddlemyer, Anne, ed. *Theatre Business: The Correspondence of the first Abbey Theatre Directors*, Gerrards Cross, 1982.

Saddlemyer, Anne, and Colin Smythe, eds. *Lady Gregory: Fifty Years After*, Gerrards Cross, 1987.

Synge, John M. *The Complete Works*, New York, 1935.

Toomey, Deirdre, ed. *Yeats and Women*, London, 1997.

Yeats, W.B. *Autobiography*, London, 1938.

Yeats, W.B. *Collected Plays*, London, 1935.

Yeats, W.B. *Collected Poems*, London, 1950.

Acknowledgments

This book was written while I was a Fellow at the Center for Scholars and Writers at the New York Public Library. I am grateful to Peter Gay, the Director, and to Pamela Leo and Rachael Kafrissen for their kindness and support. I am also grateful to my colleagues at the Center for much fruitful discussion and a great deal of stimulation.

The Lady Gregory papers are housed in the Berg Collection at the New York Public Library. My work there was greatly facilitated by Steve Crook and Isaac Gewirtz, and indeed by all the librarians who manage to make the Berg such a uniquely hospitable institution. During my time there, Declan Kiely, who was working on the Yeats papers, offered me daily assistance in deciphering Lady Gregory's handwriting, which is notoriously difficult, as well as offering much advice on the general context and background. I am also grateful to Catriona Crowe, Fintan O'Toole, and my editor at Lilliput in Dublin, Brendan Barrington.

OTHER PICADOR BOOKS
AVAILABLE FROM PAN MACMILLAN

COLM TÓIBÍN

THE SOUTH	0 330 32333 4	£6.99
THE HEATHER BLAZING	0 330 32125 0	£6.99
THE STORY OF THE NIGHT	0 330 34018 2	£6.99
THE BLACKWATER LIGHTSHIP	0 330 38986 6	£6.99
HOMAGE TO BARCELONA	0 330 37356 0	£7.99
THE SIGN OF THE CROSS	0 330 37357 9	£6.99
LOVE IN A DARK TIME	0 330 49138 5	£7.99

All Pan Macmillan titles can be ordered from our website,
www.panmacmillan.com, or from your local bookshop
and are also available by post from:

Bookpost, PO Box 29, Douglas, Isle of Man IM99 1BQ
Credit cards accepted. For details:
Telephone: 01624 677237
Fax: 01624 670923
E-mail: bookshop@enterprise.net
www.bookpost.co.uk

Free postage and packing in the United Kingdom

Prices shown above were correct at the time of going to press.
Pan Macmillan reserve the right to show new retail prices on covers
which may differ from those previously advertised in the text
or elsewhere.